Peking

Peking

Felix Greene

Photographs by Felix Greene and Yu Ma

JONATHAN CAPE
THIRTY BEDFORD SQUARE LONDON

To Anne, our daughter, who has so often
wandered with us across distant parts of China

First published 1978
© 1978 by Felix Greene
Designed by Adrienne Gear

Jonathan Cape Ltd, 30 Bedford Square, London WC1

British Library Cataloguing in Publication Data

Greene, Felix
Peking.
1. Peking – Description
I. Title
915.11′56′045   DS795
ISBN 0–224–01413–7

All the photographs in this book are by Felix Greene and
Yu Ma, with the exception of the following, for which we
gratefully acknowledge permission to reproduce: the
Library of Congress, Washington (pp. 41, centre left; 47,
top left; 49, left); the Danish Museum of Art,
Copenhagen (p. 41, bottom right); the Freer Gallery of
Art, Washington (p. 47, top right); the John Hillelson
Agency (p. 56, top); the Hsinhua News Agency, China
(pp. 31, top and centre; 56, bottom right); the Mansell
Collection (p. 49, right); the Radio Times Hulton Picture
Library (pp. 41, top; 47, bottom; 56, bottom left).

Printed in Great Britain by
Jolly & Barber Ltd, Rugby, Warwickshire

Contents

NOTE

I have followed the newer form (*Pin Yin*) for transcribing Chinese names into the English equivalents, except where the names as previously written are so familiar to Western readers that to use the new form might only be confusing.

F.G.

1 *Arrival*

The flaps are down and our 707 (1,900 kilometres non-stop from Canton) begins its long descent. I close my book and look around. Elena and I look at each other excitedly – our journey is nearly at its end. Some fellow-passengers are dozing, some are crowded at windows hoping, before the twilight fades, to catch a glimpse of the Great Wall or the first scattered lights of Peking itself. The majority of the passengers are Chinese and appear to be as excited as the rest of us. The plane is identical to all the other Boeings we have ever travelled in – the same soft lighting, the safely neutral decor, the same steady purr of the great engines. There's a disproportion here that faintly disturbs me – the vast wealth and mechanical ingenuity that lie behind the making of this plane and the stark simplicity and age-old culture of the land below us ... But that is a thought that can wait to be unravelled at a more propitious time.

Flying in this machine is too prosaic for this particular adventure. We are not heading for New York or London – we are Marco Polos about to arrive at what is still one of the remotest cities in the civilized world. Somewhere at the back of my mind, and of course absurdly, lies the thought that such an undertaking should have demanded greater dangers and more exertion. We should be arriving on foot or camel-back, dusty and travel-weary after heroic struggles. How preposterous – arriving at the Celestial City in a Boeing jet!

I think back on my other arrivals. I've lost count of the number of times I have journeyed here, but no visit has ever been the same as any other. I never fail, when approaching Peking, to experience a heightened sense of being at the very edge of a new adventure. Always when there, I find my mind enlivened, stretched, sometimes hopelessly puzzled, by a civilization that is so unlike our own. In Peking questions always crowd in faster than they can be answered; I find myself confronted with a host of new ideas, by incomprehensible disparities and concepts that challenge my most comfortable Western assumptions. To be in Peking is always enormously exciting.

1

We are still losing altitude, and now far off I can see what must be the lights of the city. You should never rush to Peking as we are doing now. I preferred the days of the little prop planes that would stop here and there on the way, and take all day, and which at some convenient airport would wait for the passengers to finish a leisurely meal. Most enjoyable of all were the journeys by train – still to be recommended as the best way of approaching Peking for those who have the time. For a day and a half you can watch China rolling by – the peasants in the fields, the planting and harvesting of rice, the huddled villages – and at the same time enjoy the finest train meals in the world.

The 'no smoking' signs come on – in Chinese characters (and in English too, but as an afterthought). A girl invites us over the intercom to fasten ourselves in. We are low now but still moving fast. Now the runway lights flash by fast as a strobe, and then at last the gentle bump and rumble as the wheels touch ground, and the swoosh of the engines in reverse as they bring the plane almost to a stop for the slow swing round towards the airport terminal. In the plane there is a sound like a collective sigh – Ah, so we're here.

Through the plane window I can see the usual group of welcomers waiting on the tarmac. It is an old Peking tradition (from years and years before the age of jets) that arrivals and departures are never treated casually but as important, almost ritual, occasions. Few Chinese and virtually no foreigners ever arrive or leave without friends or family (and in the case of a stranger, an official or two) to welcome them or see them off. Once I arrived at Peking airport in mid-winter, at midnight. Snow flurries were whipping across the runways – but there, as always, were the welcoming friends waiting outside the terminal in the biting wind, waving and smiling as our plane came to its final stop.

Now, too, friends have come to welcome the passengers – and there are some to welcome Elena and myself.

After the bear-hugs and handshakes we move inside and upstairs to the large waiting-room. We settle ourselves in leather chairs while girls come round with tea. The portrait of Mao, the great red slogans, the friendliness, the mugs of tea – all familiar and unchanged. Yes, I say to myself, we're really here!

Where else in the world does one experience this overpowering sense of having reached some ultimate destination? Not at Kennedy or Heathrow or De Gaulle – they are just staging points from which passengers hustle off again in all directions. It's all bustle and grab, a struggle for bags and porters and taxis; an anonymous maelstrom of people all hoping to get going as quickly as possible on their individual ways. And here — what a contrast! — passengers and friends sit sipping tea while somewhere passports are being checked and luggage is carried out to waiting cars. And — blessed thought — no worry about how much to tip. No one fusses and no one hurries. And why hurry? For this is Peking, the end of the line, and who wants to hurry on from here? Perhaps those arriving at Rome in ancient times felt this same sense of finality, for that city also in its day was the ultimate focal point of a vast area of the known world. It's not an accident that long ago in China they also coined a saying (as every Chinese child will tell you) that 'All roads lead to Peking'.

We are staying at the Hsin Chiao Hotel. I'm up early the next morning and hurry downstairs. There's no sound in the hotel; the lobby, half in darkness, is deserted except for an attendant sorting papers behind the front desk. He glances up to give me a good-morning nod.

Out into the cool air. The sky is cloudless and the first glow of sunrise is spreading across the eastern horizon. The Peking dawn in the early spring has a quality of colour all its own — a pearly translucence difficult to describe. On the rare occasions when I have seen a similar dawn — in Mexico, perhaps, or Arizona — I recognize it at once: there in the sky is an unmistakable Peking dawn.

I walk on, turning right where Chungwenmen once stood — one of the high three-tiered gates through the city wall. Years ago I watched a train of camels pass through that gate, noses in the air and with that appearance of supreme disdain that only camels can achieve. They were arriving with merchandise from far away. But that was twenty years ago. Today trucks and not camels bring goods from distant places, and the wall and the gate have gone too.

I walk to the section of Peking that used to be known as the Chinese City. The sun is up now and the streets have come alive. Buses, some driven by young women and jammed with early workers, toot incessantly and with not the slightest effect, at myriad bicyclists who weave across the street. Rush hour in Peking means bicycle time, bicycles by the tens of thousands. There are $2\frac{1}{2}$ million of them in Peking.

I notice two old men walking with great dignity, hands tucked in their sleeves and deep in quiet talk. Seeing me, a foreigner, they bow gravely as they pass. Trucks stacked high with vegetables and fruit rumble by on their way to the central markets. Outside one grocery shop I have to step around cabbages and cucumbers piled high on the pavement, unsold from the previous day. A single piece of string tied between two bamboo sticks has guarded them overnight. A woman now removes it indicating that she is open for business.

I turn west into a veritable maze of little alleys – the famous *hutungs* of Peking. There are no fewer than 2,800 of these small lanes, most of them too narrow for anything much wider than a handcart. It is here, in these *hutungs*, that old Peking survives largely untouched by the massive modern construction that is going on elsewhere.

The walls on either side of these lanes are unbroken except for doorways. No windows look out on to these tiny streets, for the houses turn inwards upon themselves, with rooms built around a courtyard. The dominant colour in the *hutungs* is grey, the colour of the indigenous clay. The walls are of grey brick, the tiles on the curved roofs are grey, even the street itself is grey. Only over some of the doorways is there a little colour – a row of bright tiles; or now, in spring, an occasional spray of green rising from a tree behind a wall. And if you should pass an entrance while the door is open, you will catch a glimpse of the tiny courtyard ablaze with potted flowers.

The houses in the *hutungs* are low, never more than a single storey. Centuries ago an emperor decreed that Peking was to remain a one-storeyed city so that no citizen could inflict the indignity of looking down on him if he, the Son of Heaven, were ever carried by in his palanquin. I walk zig-zag from one small alley to the next, losing my way, but hopefully going in the right direction. Outside several houses women are sprinkling water on the road and then carefully sweeping the dust in front of their gates. A girl on a bicycle stops to knock on this door and that to deliver newspapers and at each stop there is an exchange of greeting 'Ni hao!' – 'How are you?'

At one time houses of one storey, with rooms around a patio, must have seemed a sensible and convenient arrangement to the people of Peking – in fact the only sensible way to build a house. Why extend houses into the sky? As recently as the eighteenth century, the Emperor Kang-hsi, when he was shown pictures of European houses, exclaimed: 'Undoubtedly this Europe must be a very small and pitiful Country since the Inhabitants cannot find Ground enough to spread out their Towns but are obliged to live thus up in the Air.'

The *hutungs* are now smoky with breakfast fires. A group of people are gathered round a vendor of fried bean curd, a father squats on his heels to feed his small boy. The morning is full of varied sounds – a rooster crowing, a motor starting up in a machine shop, somewhere the rasping of a hand-saw. Two boys, arm in arm but with hands in pockets and satchels on their back, are strolling towards me on their way to

Leaving the newspaper office for the morning delivery.

Bus journey during the Peking rush hour.

A *hutung* courtyard.

school. One of them sees me and nudges the other. They stop their talk and watch me as they approach, half curiously, half warily. (Foreigners are still, especially to children, something of a curiosity.) '*Ni hao!*' I say. '*Ni hao! Ni hao!*' they call back, and run off giggling.

I have walked farther than I thought and unexpectedly I find myself out of the *hutungs* and in a main thoroughfare, now thronged with people and loud with tooting buses and trucks. These first-morning walks in old Peking – almost a ritual with me now – help me to change my mental gears, to slow down, to shed the West a little. The chatter of Chinese voices all around me, the strange shrill music from loud speakers, the immense red billboard at the intersection with its slogan SERVE THE PEOPLE – all remind me that I'm no longer in Piccadilly; but for a few days there will linger a sense of unreality, as if some part of me hasn't yet arrived.

I should get back to the hotel, but stand for a few moments to watch the people in this busy street. Some are obviously going to work; women with their string bags are off to do the morning shopping. Nearly all are in quilted blue, for it's not yet warm enough for the brighter clothes of summer. I notice that in spite of their number, they make no noise as they walk, no clatter of shoes, for they still wear the traditional soft slippers. Even soldiers more often than not wear gym shoes.

I watch one lady moving through the crowd. She's tiny and rather stooped. She is dressed, like all old women are, in black trousers and a black tunic drawn up to one shoulder and buttoned down the side. Her grey hair is pulled back and tied in a small knot behind her head, emphasizing her high cheek bones and a face lined by age. Beside her, supporting her by the elbow, is a tall girl of about eighteen, clear-eyed and self-confident, probably her grand-daughter. The old lady walks with an awkward, shuffling gait, for her feet are minute, perhaps ten centimetres long – a legacy from the barbaric days of foot-binding. One rarely sees these mutilated feet in Peking today and only on the very old, yet seeing this I am reminded again with a shock how recently China has emerged from her feudal past. There they are, side by side, representatives of the old China and the new.

As I stroll back, I think of the people of Peking. They appear so comfortable in their loose baggy clothes and their soft shoes. There's no vanity here, no 'fashion', no concern for mere appearance. They are comfortable with themselves, comfortable and casual with each other. So much so that visitors often feel they have stepped into a single, large family. Which is not true, of course. As we know, they have their times

Chienmen Street; Chienmen was the main gate that once divided the
Inner from the Outer City.

of violence and bitter struggle. They are not meek, these people of
Peking. They must be among the most genuinely courteous and gener-
ous people in the world. If they count you as a friend and you're in need,
they will give their last shirt to you without a thought. But try to deceive
them, try to cheat or humiliate them, or cross them on an issue that they
consider a matter of principle and you will find, below their composure
and gentleness, just how strong and passionate they are. Yet, watching
them now as I walk back to my hotel, I can see no sign of tension or
anxiety or hurry.

The people of Peking! Unhurried, undistinguishable, indestruct-
ible – the inheritors of almost 4,000 years of unbroken cultural continuity. There was a city on this spot before London was anything
more than a collection of mud huts. China was never influenced
by the great Greek and Roman civilizations, or by Christendom.
Thus separated by distance and culture, two streams of civilization evolved over many thousands of years virtually unknown to each

other. China and Europe might almost have been on different planets. No wonder, then, the social customs of the Chinese, their concepts of law and democracy, their art, their relatedness to nature, their manners, their writing, the very processes of their thinking are so different from our own. It is this very 'differentness' that provides the appeal that has attracted and baffled the imaginations of generations of travellers, ever since the first European 'discovered' China more than 700 years ago. It must be this attraction of the 'unknown' that has excited almost every one who has ever travelled to Peking so that for the rest of their lives they are left with a lingering nostalgia. It cannot be the historical buildings, for other countries have them too; and apart from them, and the temples, Peking is, as cities go, one of the more drab and dusty. Nor can it be the climate that appeals, for Peking is bitterly cold in winter, savagely hot in summer.

I have known Western newspaper correspondents stationed in Peking, tough-minded and sceptical, frustrated almost beyond bearing by the restrictions imposed by Chinese officialdom, counting the days until their transfer elsewhere. But they have not reckoned on Peking's subtle spell. After a few months in London or Tokyo or Timbuktoo they have begun to send out feelers as to when they can hope to be sent to Peking again.

Peking and her people fascinate me for quite other reasons. People in London, Paris, Rome – even in New York – by and large have a nostalgia for the past. The golden age was then, not today; and certainly not in any conceivable future. So Westerners tend to cling to quaint customs not because they are useful but simply because they are old; they still love to see soldiers parade in shining armour; they retain absurd legal fictions, dress up in wigs, draw up contracts written in medieval language, maintain political procedures which everyone knows are largely sham. And clinging to the past, anything new is frightening.

Not so in Peking. Here people have no nostalgia for the past. It is the present and the future that they thrill to. Peking is above all a revolutionary city, full of revolutionary experimentation. There is nothing going on in Peking that is not in some sense political, for the people there are altering the very foundation of their society. That is why there is no other city like it in the world.

These were my thoughts as I walked back to the hotel.

The lobby which was empty when I left is now full of people – all kinds of people of many different nationalities. There are tourists carrying cameras and interpreters standing by ready to take them on excursions to the Summer Palace or the tombs of the Ming emperors;

8

members of the hotel staff bring lunch-boxes from the kitchen for guests going to the Great Wall; Indians in saris and handsome black Africans from the Cameroons; a team of football players from Yugoslavia; and Japanese — lots of them — each with an identical 'executive' brief case, waiting to be driven to business offices. And by the front door (for it's still too cold for them to be outside) are the taxi drivers — rugged-faced, easy-going, and utterly unconcerned with all the activity around them. Through the swing door comes a messenger from the cable office; he empties a leather bag full of the morning's telegrams on to the front desk and he waits until they are logged before he leaves.

Out of the lift step several girls, pert in their blue Air France uniforms. Beautifully made-up — the lips just the right red, the eye-shadow just the right blue — they appear incongruous, so odd can make-up seem in China. The Russians, all men, Aeroflot crews are something else again, short and broad-shouldered, in dark blue, gold braid and peaked caps, faces stern and watchful; they have the look of men who feel they are in enemy country.

This scene is not at all representative of Peking, since only four of the city's 187 hotels are set aside for foreign visitors. The new Peking Hotel is the most luxurious but the Hsin Chiao is the liveliest and most friendly, and remains our favourite.

Peking is not a cosmopolitan city. There are times, quite probably, when more visitors arrive in New York or London in a week than arrive in Peking in the course of a whole year. This makes one all the more aware of the differences between the people of Peking and the visitors from elsewhere. These hotel guests can be readily identified and categorized without their uttering a word. But step outside into the street and try to identify the people of Peking. That man approaching — does he work in a bank or in a factory? And if in a factory, is he the general manager or the man who sweeps the factory floor? There is no way of telling — not by his looks or his speech or his clothes. Even the uniformed soldier, for all one can tell, could be an officer or a new recruit.

I go up to my room. Elena is awake and ready for breakfast. London now seems a million miles away. I'm here. I'm in Peking. I feel deeply content.

2 Peking Day by Day

Three Chinese will be looking after us during our twelve-week stay.

Ch'i Ming-tsung, a senior and experienced member of the Information Department of the Foreign Ministry, is an old friend. He accompanied Elena, our daughter Anne and me for several months in 1972 when we were filming in many far-off places in China and in 1976 he was with us while filming in Tibet. Ch'i was at the London embassy for some years, speaks impeccable English and knows enough about our awkward Western ways to be able in an unobtrusive way to guide us through any social difficulties. He is a vegetarian, which pleases Elena who is one too. Photography (when he has the time to pursue it) is one of his hobbies and he possesses a nice mechanical sense which at times, when equipment breaks down, has come in very useful. In places where people have never been photographed by foreigners before he has an authoritative but always kindly way of reassuring them that we are really quite harmless. Ch'i is always ready with a laugh. In brief, a very good companion to have around. Alas, on this trip he will not be able to be with us often. The growing number of foreign correspondents in Peking are always seeking his help as well.

Then Yu Ma. (He is the son of an old friend of mine, Dr George Ma Hai-teh, who is an American of Syrian extraction, has lived in China since before the Revolution and has contributed enormously to the development of China's medical services.) Yu Ma is a photographer on the magazine *China Reconstructs* and many of the pictures in this book are his. I could not have wished for a better or more willing photographer-companion. Yu Ma speaks no English but, as fellow-photographers, we developed as we worked a system of non-verbal communication which was as good as language.

When Elena first met Lü Feng-ting – the third Chinese member of our team – she said, 'Surely we have met before.' Lü smiled and said he didn't think so. Several times after that I would catch Elena looking at Lü and shaking her head, puzzled. 'I *have* met Lü *somewhere*,' she would say, 'I know I have, but I can't think where.'

10

Dawn over the
Imperial City.

Tending plants in a
hutung courtyard.

Children on their way to school.

Morning in Peking: shopping in a street market.

Ch'i Ming-tsung   Yu Ma   Lü Feng-ting

Weeks later, going through the Palace Museum with Yu Ma and Lü, we stopped to admire once again one of our favourite small statues in gilded bronze – the figure of a young man on his knees holding a lamp of 'eternal fidelity'. It was made in the early Han dynasty, over 2,000 years ago. Yu Ma touched my arm and pointed to the statue and then to Lü. The likeness was extraordinary, startling. Then Elena saw it, 'Ah,' she exclaimed excitedly, 'there you are, Lü – I *knew* we had met before!' She won her point at last.

Lü was our very excellent interpreter, modest, charming and always cheerful. We never once saw him in anything but a good humour, even when I was at my testiest and most impatient. He does not normally act as an interpreter but he never seemed to be at a loss for a word. I hope that on any future journey he will be with us again.

So there we were, Ch'i Ming-tsung, Yu Ma, Lü, Elena and myself, in our hotel bedroom making our plans – and before we had finished they had agreed to all our suggestions and before our work was over they had arranged visits for us to no fewer than eighty-two different places in and around Peking.

We know from experience that it takes time to make the necessary arrangements. Schools, factories, theatres, communes, will need to be contacted and told that one day strangers slung with cameras may walk in; time and days have to be determined and cars arranged. Elena and I are both glad of the delay, for it needs more than a walk through the *hutungs* to feel at home again in Peking.

We visit old friends who tell us what changes have taken place since we were here last; but mostly, free of all pressure, we use these days to stroll through the streets, visiting familiar places, exploring new ones. We stand again in wonder at the sheer artistry and magnificence of the ancient palaces, and the Temple of Heaven, one of the most perfect examples of Ming architecture. Every morning, usually without set plan, we are content to saunter through the streets, for in no other city can one see so great an interplay between people, so many tiny human happenings or be among a people who are at once so relaxed, and yet convey such a vivid sense of vitality. Out of habit I carry a camera, but hardly use it. That can come later. These days, before serious work begins, provide an opportunity just to watch.

One day, however, we do have a plan. We rise early, 5.30 – already too late for sunrise – and catch a No. 303 trolley-bus that takes us to the North Gate of the Forbidden City, the entrance to what is now known as the Palace Museum. The gate, of course, is still closed at this hour, but today the museum isn't our objective. Around the Forbidden City is a wide, water-filled moat. Between this moat and the high wall of the Forbidden City is a space, perhaps thirty paces wide, that runs the entire length of the northern wall, nearly a kilometre in length. In this area between wall and moat, thousands of willow trees have been planted. We cross the bridge and here, under these slender willows, we enter a wholly different world. Peking is changing fast, and the people's social attitudes have undergone a profound revolution, but some old customs remain as alive as ever. Very early every morning, as they have done for years, people who wish to practise their particular skill come to this place – young men and old, girls, schoolboys, students, musicians, singers. Nothing is formalized and no one interferes. Some have come alone, some with friends. They pay little attention to each other, for everyone is absorbed in his own activity. There is no noisy chatter. When people speak, we notice they do so quietly.

Here three old men are moving through the slow, stylized patterns of a sword dance. There a young boy stands playing a violin with his music propped against a tree. A little further we find six very young boys practising acrobatics and, even at their age, doing so with terrific vitality and precision. I walk over to a student sitting on the low wall that overlooks the moat. Coming close, I see that the book he is engrossed in is a French grammar. *'Parlez-vous français?'* I ask, and he looks up startled and then breaks into a smile. *'Non, non ... un petit peu ...'* he stumbles, a little embarrassed.

We walk on – a man doing Tai Chi Chuan arrests our attention and

12

we stop to watch him. His movements are superbly controlled, his body unstrained, his face with half-closed eyes utterly composed – it is a meditation in movement. Several others have joined him – they recognize a master. Taking their place behind him, first one then another begins to follow his movements until there are perhaps ten or twelve moving with his majestic rhythm. He has become their teacher. At the end of a sequence he turns and, seeing us, smiles briefly. Now, facing the group, he leads them into the next sequence. Without any affectation he accepts the role of teacher just as simply and wordlessly as they accept him. They move through the stages of the sequence and now he watches them, giving a suggestion here, a word of encouragement there.

From far down the long wall comes the voice of a woman rehearsing the strange, high-pitched singing of Peking opera; nearer, we hear the pure notes of a flute. The water, the early translucent light filtering through the leaves, the medley of sounds, the silent movements of the people around us, blend into a scene of extraordinary calm and beauty. We stand entranced. I finger my camera, but then leave it slung across my back. This is their world, why should I intrude with mine?

Later, I mention my reticence to Lü. He ponders unhurriedly, searching for a way to explain without hurting my feelings. 'Yes, you see with us the taking of photographs is always a private thing, between members of a family or close friends. So you were right, your camera, if you had used it, would probably have disturbed them. Perhaps another morning we will go together and I can reassure them that you are a friend.'

So a few days later we returned and Lü came with us. The same magic atmosphere, the same variety of activities and sounds. As we walked slowly under the trees Lü would murmur a few words to this group or to that individual, and then nod to me indicating 'It's all right', and I (still feeling something of an intruder) would take a few photographs. Only one old man quietly shook his head; the others, reassured, seemed hardly to notice that we were there.

In Peking, to be vouched for as a friend opens many doors.

Not far from Chienmen – one of the oldest and grandest of the three-tiered gates – is a favourite Peking street of mine branching off to the right from Chienmen Street. This street is in old Peking and many of the shop fronts are decorated with intricate lattice work. The street is not wide enough for cars so it tends to be always full of pedestrians and young children, who enjoy looking at the toy shops. In this street you can buy groceries, clothes, toys, ice-cream, musical instruments, foot-

Early morning: learning Tai Chi Chuan
from a master.

Buying sweets in one of
Peking's large department stores.

Water melons piled high along Peking's main shopping street.

balls, big red lanterns – almost anything. We much prefer to shop here than in Wangfujing, the main shopping street of Peking, and we prefer it infinitely to the 'Friendship Store', a shiny modern establishment set up exclusively for foreigners.

Today we have come to Lang Fang To Chiao to buy, among other things, some bamboo flutes for a boy in California. The flutes we are shown in the music shop are exquisitely made and polished. There are many kinds of flutes. 'Try them,' the shop assistant suggests, 'for they all vary a little.' Neither of us can play a flute so we ask him to choose the best. Very carefully he examines the flutes, playing a few notes on each. He finally separates several. *'Hen hao'* ('These are very good'). I nod and he deftly wraps them, each flute in its own box. From the care he has taken one might think that we have chosen some expensive instrument. In fact these bamboo flutes cost only 10p each.

This same attention is given us in every shop we go to, even in the busy department stores and markets. The weather is warmer now, and before long Peking will be very hot indeed. I'm looking for a shop where I can buy a pair of the loose and shapeless trousers which will be worn by almost everyone. They are spacious, cool and wonderfully comfortable.

We find the shop, and moving to the counter we try, as we always do, to stand unobtrusively in line behind those already waiting to be served. And, as always, it doesn't work. The attendant sees us and the people in front of us move aside. No one appears annoyed that we have jumped the queue, rather they stand fascinated and crowd around us to see what these foreigners are about to buy. 'Trousers,' I say in Chinese and the attendant brings out a selection of smart dress trousers. *'Bu, bu,'* I say, 'No, no.' He looks puzzled and there is a momentary impasse. The people around us ask questions which we cannot understand, and trying to be helpful they tell the attendant to bring other trousers, for perhaps those he showed me are not quite good enough. How can I explain? I spot a man who is wearing exactly the kind of trousers I am looking for and I beckon him to the counter. *'These!'* I say, pointing to the bewildered man. There is a babble of chatter and laughter. Does the foreigner really intend to wear *Chinese* trousers? The people and the shop attendant suddenly look at us with a new kind of friendliness. They stay gathered around us while the trousers are neatly wrapped and they smile their goodbyes as we begin to move away. As we have found so often, it doesn't need words to make friends in China.

It's water melon time in Peking. Literally millions of these huge green gourds are stacked along the streets, sometimes with matting over them to protect them from the summer sun. All day long loaded carts and trucks come in from the Communes, renewing supplies. Peking people have a passion for these melons. They are very sweet and very cheap – 10 or 12 *fen* a kilo. (About 3p, 5½¢.) Along all the main shopping streets long stands have been set up for those who want to eat them on the spot. The stands are ingeniously constructed with a trough into which one spits the seeds and, behind, a container for the rinds. It's a great sight – old men and women, boys, girls, toddlers hardly able to walk – all tucking in. Even the babies in their wicker pushchairs are given little chunks.

With our two parcels we stroll down the street. In a shop window we notice a colourful poster showing three young women tackling different kinds of work. 'TIMES HAVE CHANGED!' the caption reads. 'MEN AND WOMEN ARE NOW EQUAL. CRITICIZE THE IDEA THAT MEN ARE SUPERIOR TO WOMEN!'

It is difficult to discard old attitudes, especially the idea, so deeply ingrained that males are inherently superior to women. For 2,300 years Confucius directed the Chinese people to 'Remain in your place and submit to the laws of heaven'. Daughters, he said, must submit to their fathers; wives must submit to their husbands; widows must submit to their eldest son. Confucius' teaching, with emphasis on ceremony, ritual, procedures, was designed to maintain the status quo. Very convenient for men and for the ruling élite. No wonder there was a national campaign against the old sage whose words were accepted almost as law for so many centuries; and against 'old ideas, old culture, old customs, old habits'. Since 1949, when the revolutionary government took over, women have enjoyed legal equality with men, and to a considerable extent they have achieved it. But age-old attitudes don't vanish just because of laws. So they keep the reminders going.

A little further down the street there is another poster which neither of us had seen before. A young couple, just married or about to be, are surrounded by smiling family and friends. 'TIMES HAVE CHANGED!' says the caption. 'MARRY IN THE NEW WAY AND PRACTISE FAMILY PLANNING WELL!'

Times have indeed changed. What a revolution in attitude lies behind these posters – and what a struggle.

It's lunch time now and we're hungry. We walk back to Chienmen Street and into the nearest restaurant.

It's a small place, and very crowded and there appears to be no table free. We are just about to share one with a young couple when an attendant comes and politely asks the young people to move to the next table so that we can have one to ourselves. They do so willingly. A pity. We would rather have sat with them. But this is the normal practice in restaurants where foreigners are concerned. The intention is kindly, not to 'isolate' one from the Chinese people. They feel we prefer it this way.

The people notice us and many glance our way. It is unlikely that many foreigners come to this small place. It's full of workers, women with children, a couple of P.L.A. men (People's Liberation Army), a policeman, office workers and a few who are clearly from the country and in Peking for a holiday. It's a restaurant, as the Chinese would put it, 'for the masses'. There's lots of lively chatter.

Our table, covered with a coloured plastic cloth, is wiped clean and we give our order – two large plates of *jiaozi* (small dumplings filled with vegetables) and I walk over to a counter for two glasses of draught beer. We can see a cauldron of *jiaozi* already cooked and steaming from which others are being served, but we are not given these. The cooks have been told, 'This order is for foreign friends', and they insist on cooking fresh ones for us. Again, kindly meant but we wish they had not bothered. Now two children, toddlers, have crept towards our table to study us. 'Hullo,' says Elena. No response. '*Ni hao,*' I say. Still no response. They remain expressionless and wide-eyed, absorbed in their examination of these strange humans with big noses and blue eyes.

The *jiaozi* when they come are delicious and more than enough for a meal. While we eat I tell Elena about a delegation of foreign journalists who were visiting Peking last week. Some of them wanted to experience the very ultimate in Peking cuisine and they sent a message to one of the stylish restaurants that is mostly used by overseas visitors: 'Please prepare dinner for nine people tomorrow night, the very best food, regardless of the cost.' (On expense accounts of course!) The chef took them at their word. The next evening they ate like the ancient emperors. They had elaborate hors d'œuvres including cold duck marinated in wine; *yin er* (a white fungus cooked in chicken oil); *yin si juan* (buns with silver threads); *yan wo* (sea swallows' nests); *xiang ji chi* (aromatic crisp chicken); prawns fried with ginger, and many other exotic delicacies, including *salmon* fin – a dish even more rare than sharks' fin. All this was washed down with *mao tai* (a strong colourless spirit distilled from wheat and millet) and Chinese wines. The bill, I was told, was enormous.

Now our bill comes – totalling 15 *fen* each, including the beer – not quite 5p (9½¢)!

Between a simple eating place such as ours and the journalists' fancy

17

restaurant, there are more than 1,013 restaurants to choose from in Peking. Restaurants of every size and style and for every pocket; restaurants specializing in the local food of China's provinces; all-night restaurants for workers on late shifts; wine bars and snack bars – the variety is endless. There are Mongolian restaurants where, on a brazier brought to the table, one can cook one's own meat. One of the best meals I ever had in Peking was in a restaurant where you first bought your meat and vegetables at the counter and then cooked them yourself above a huge communal charcoal fire set in the middle of the room. Today the *jiaozi* and beer suited us well enough and we walk back to our hotel well satisfied.

Back at the hotel, walking down the fourth floor corridor to our room, we hear a voice that is both familiar and strange. We stop for a moment to listen. A radio; yes, and the voice is unquestionably English. We explore and find the floor attendant sitting at his table, head in his hands, his eyes following the words in a book before him – a picture of despairing concentration. From a radio the voice rolls on slowly and inexorably, each word too precisely enunciated on its own: 'And where did you go for your vacation?' And another voice answers with the same deliberation, 'I spent my vacation in a commune working with the peasants. It was a very good ...'

The young attendant senses our presence and looks up. Shaking his head, he says, *'Yingwen hen bu rong yi.'* We heartily agree with him, and then I say it slowly in English for him to repeat: 'The English language is very difficult!'

'English by radio.' In recent years, tens of millions of Chinese have been listening to these broadcasts, trying to master this alien speech. The radio station in Peking receives hundreds of letters every week from taxi drivers, shop assistants, workers in factories, peasants in the surrounding country. Once, when the station temporarily broke down and that day's English programme was missed, an enormous number of listeners wrote in, urgently requesting that the lesson be repeated.

This curiosity, this wish to learn something new and also to see how things work, one meets everywhere. I need only stop to change a film in my camera and before I know it half a dozen young men and women will be at my elbow to watch me. I notice that any happening in the street, be it only the digging of a pipe-line or the pruning of a tree, will always draw a fascinated crowd.

Walking through the Forbidden City, Elena and I noticed again how aware Peking people are of the past – the Palace Museums are always crowded, and any new archaeological discoveries are widely reported and eagerly discussed. I remember Richard Harris, who speaks Chinese, describing how he once stood in line to buy a ticket at Peking railway station and he overheard a conversation of two Chinese soldiers who were standing in the line too. They had apparently been taking part in military manoeuvres and were discussing whether or not the strategies that had been followed were in accordance with the theories of Sunzi – a brilliant military writer who lived around 500 B.C. I don't think that a British or American soldier would know the name of *any* military strategist, let alone be able to discuss his theories, let alone if he lived 2,500 years ago. The answer I think lies in a different concept of what 'history' means. To most Westerners, history refers only to something that is past, finished, gone, done with, dead. The Chinese, however, regard history as a flow, a movement, so the past is never dead because it includes the present and the future too. They see today as history, and it is linked to yesterday and is linked to tomorrow too ...

Once, while talking with the late Premier Chou En-lai, I was asking him questions about Taiwan and he said, 'You Westerners are always in such a hurry, you want things to happen right away. Taiwan is part of China, and we will go on pressing for it, and one day it will be united with us again ... it might be in five years, or ten or fifty. What is certain is that it will one day be liberated, that is what really matters.' A different sense of time ...

A few days later I find a fault in one of my cameras so I walk over to Wangfujing, to a small camera-repair shop I have used before. The man there takes my camera and gently removes the lens and back. He examines it carefully, then looks up. *'Hao'* – 'Come back in half an hour.'

There's a railing near the department store and I sit on that, quite content to watch what goes on. I never tire of the people that fill the pavements of Peking. I watch them now, each one going about his business with an air – what is it? – a serenity, an extraordinary absence of anxiety. Perhaps *security* is the better word, secure in themselves and secure in the knowledge that nothing can harm them. I suddenly realize how secure I feel too. Here I am, a stranger in a crowded city, virtually unable to speak the language, yet with complete certainty that if I were suddenly to fall ill or be hurt by a passing car, a hundred people would at once surround me and arrange for whatever help I needed. And it occurs to me too that it was only last night that Elena and I walked home at midnight from the house of a friend, down many dimly lit streets, and the thought of possible *danger* never so much as crossed our minds.

I see a whole family across the street, sitting in a circle on the pavement, enjoying ice cream as unconcernedly as if they were in a park. Children near by are running freely here and there, a boy chases another round a tree, and further away I can see a group of children having the time of their lives on a pile of sand that has been unloaded in the street.

I realize again how closely the Chinese relate to each other. True enough, during the rush hour they scramble and push to get on to a crowded bus as vigorously as do people in London or Paris. But seeing them now, they saunter rather than walk. The cars hoot incessantly with no effect as pedestrians wander at all angles across the street. School-children pass by, red scarves around their necks and arms round each other, full of excited chatter; an endless stream of shoppers with string bags, babies in wicker push-chairs or on their mothers' backs, grand-mothers, soldiers, workers. A policeman, white-jacketed, strolls among the people and stops to chat with a man unloading cabbages.

How astonishingly young these Peking policemen look! As in Bri-tain, they are unarmed. They are, as it were, part of the family — no wariness between them and the people. Only their white jackets give them a certain, rather tentative appearance of authority. But, as with so many things in Peking, appearances can be deceptive. These police may be young and unarmed but they are a highly trained force and in superb physical condition. Their real strength lies in their relationship with the people and the respect in which they are held. They are trained to think of themselves as serving the public, and — as with the soldiers — I have never seen a policeman sitting in a crowded bus if a civilian has to stand.

Here, in one of the world's largest cities, the people have some-how retained the sense of community one might expect to find in a small town. They do not have the living standards of the West but they have no *class* poverty. Everyone belongs, no one is left out. I have yet to see, in all my visits here, a beggar or a human derelict or, for that matter, a drunk.

What a rich scene this is, this never-ending movement of the people in their soft shoes and their loose comfortable clothes. This woman, near by, sweeping the streets. I watch her as she gathers what little débris there is — there's very little for the main streets are washed down every night. A young girl comes down the street — I doubt if she's more than ten — carrying a baby in her arms; she pauses, expertly shifts the baby on to her back and moves on, leaning forward a little to take the weight. A very old man, bent and a little shaky, and a small lad, perhaps five years old, walk by slowly hand-in-hand. Who, I wonder, is looking after whom?

'Times have changed! Marry in the new way!'

Right, a hot summer evening.

A policeman 'serving the people'.

It's time to collect my camera. The man hands it to me and demonstrates that the problem has been solved. I thank him and ask, 'How much?' 'It was a simple matter — there's no charge.'

A friend of mine, an English doctor, is in hospital and as it's still early I walk there to visit him. He is in what is now named the Capital Hospital. Originally built with money from the Rockefeller Foundation, it was known for a long time as the Peking Union Medical College, or P.U.M.C. for short. Before the Revolution it was the only modern hospital in Peking and reserved almost entirely for foreigners and wealthy Chinese. Now, of course, there are dozens of hospitals with 23,000 fully trained doctors and 29,000 beds in all, providing a bed for every 275 citizens.

I once had a few weeks in that hospital myself. It was in winter during a very cold spell and I fell ill with pneumonia. I will never forget, during my first few days when I was lying, full of fever and antibiotics, how the nurses silently flitted in and out of the room like friendly ghosts — ministering angels perhaps would be a better way of putting it. Marvellously competent and gentle. I was rather daunted when they told me I would need three injections a day, especially when I saw the amount of antibiotics they were intending to pump into me. I need not have worried. The injections turned out to be entirely painless. This puzzled me until I asked George Ma Hai-teh (my American doctor friend) what the secret was.

'Melons,' he said.

'What do you mean, *melons?*'

'Well,' he said, 'cucumbers do almost as well.'

I thought the poor man had gone out of his mind.

'It's the nurses' training,' he went on. 'They practise giving injections on melons or cucumbers, for the skins offer about the same resistance as the human skin. They don't push the needle in, they learn to handle it like a dart. After they pass the melon stage, the nurses practise on each other until they're really good at it and only then do they inject patients.'

Among the doctors, nurses and other hospital staff, the question of status is not considered important. It surprised me when one of the most experienced doctors was quite ready to fetch water for me or take away my lunch tray. One day a young doctor needed to introduce a tiny thread-like needle into the veins of one of my hands — a delicate operation which he performed with great gentleness and skill. Ten minutes later he came back to my room with a ladder and changed the curtains!

Buses in Peking are nearly always crowded. But foreigners are hardly ever allowed to stand. As soon as Elena and I board a bus two people will invariably offer us their seats – either voluntarily or perhaps because of a quiet word from the ticket-girl. I wish they wouldn't. I have tried a number of times just to keep on standing in the hope that someone will eventually take the empty seat. But no one ever does and there is general embarrassment, so in the end, defeated, I sit down.

One day, something quite unexpected happened when we took a bus. By mistake we took a bus that did not run as far as we thought. The end of its run was about a mile from our destination. During the journey, with my few words of Chinese I struck up a hesitant conversation with the ticket-girl. She asked where we were going and I told her. Then we were interrupted by the influx of other passengers. At the end of the line all the other passengers got out and we tried to too, but the ticket-girl stopped us. She and the driver then had a brief consultation and the bus moved on – with us as the sole passengers. They took us precisely to our destination! We thanked them warmly and, as we walked away, we looked back. The bus hadn't moved – the driver and the girl were watching us; they waved goodbye and we waved back.

Why this extraordinary kindness to strangers? In this case I rather think it was because I had made some attempt, however stumbling, to communicate. These small human contacts sometimes bring surprisingly happy consequences.

One of the most widely used slogans in China – it's seen everywhere – is SERVE THE PEOPLE. The idea behind it hasn't remained just a slogan on a big board but in all sorts of ways has filtered down into all kinds of actions. One afternoon, for example, I needed a box in which to send my exposed films abroad by air freight for processing. 'The Post Office will help you,' I was told. So off I went to the office near Chienmen. 'I need a box,' I said, 'a strong one.' The girl attendant disappeared and came back with several wooden boxes, asking me to choose the size I needed. The cost was 1 *yuan* (32p; 60¢) and that included some nails as well. I told her that I wished our post offices gave the same kind of service to the public. 'Our system is different,' she said.

I saw the same slogan in action again that afternoon when I took this box, now packed, to the air freight office. After weighing it and completing all the necessary forms, the man handed me the airway bill and I noticed that all the handling charges this end, including sending this 3kg box to the airport, was just 3 *fen*, less than 1p (2¢). I pointed this out – a mistake, surely. 'No, the charge is based on our regular scale; we only charge what it costs us.'

23

Chou En-lai at the first of several interviews with the author (1960).

We have been in Peking now for two weeks and our real work has not yet started. This kind of delay irritated me when I first came to Peking many years ago. I have learned better now. When dealing with officials in Peking, nothing is said or done without deliberation. There is no such thing as official spontaneity, never an immediate 'yes' or 'no' to any suggestion one might make, but always 'We will consider it,' or 'We will let you know.' Every decision, even quite a minor one, it seems, is discussed with colleagues and carefully considered. To impatient Westerners, accustomed to quick, off-the-cuff answers, this deliberation can be exasperating. But it is also reassuring, for when a decision is finally reached it will not be an idle one which might later be reversed. When arrangements are made you know they will be followed through.

A good example of this is my first interview with the late Premier Chou En-lai. I was in Shanghai when a message reached me that the Premier was ready to see me, so I hurried back to Peking by the next train. But then nothing happened. After waiting for two weeks I asked an official whether the interview was still on. He looked at me in mild astonishment and said simply, 'The Premier agreed that he would see you.' That was all. It was more than another week before they phoned to say that on that evening Mr Chou En-lai would see me. I waited until almost midnight when an official from the Premier's office phoned and said, 'We are now sending a car for you. The Premier apologizes for having kept you so late but he has been in a Central Committee meeting until now.' I suggested that the Premier might be very tired and wouldn't he prefer to postpone our meeting to another day. 'No, he wishes to see you tonight and the car will be at your hotel very soon.'

Chou En-lai, even after a whole day's meeting, seemed alert, unhurried and quite untired. It was 2 a.m. before I said goodbye. The next day I heard that at 6 a.m. that same morning Chou En-lai had left Peking on the start of his important African tour. He had arranged to see this foreign journalist and, even though it had to be at the last minute and at a most inconvenient hour, the promise was kept.

Looking back now on all my many visits, I realize that it is not the rather dusty city or its ancient palaces and temples that come to mind when I say 'Peking'. It is the *people* that I think of — millions of them, living in one great metropolis, yet never strident, always beguilingly polite and courteous. Their manners, made mellow and urbane by time, sometimes conceal — unless one listens carefully to the nuances of their speech — what it is that they wish one to understand, and one is forever conscious of the clumsiness of one's own approach. But once you have broken through the barrier of formality it is easy to have a good time because the Chinese are not at heart a solemn people. And once they have accepted you as a friend, they will stand by you, solid as a rock.

Yet there is one, more subtle, barrier that hardly any foreigner ever crosses — he will never quite 'belong'. The Chinese have their own intimate memories of poverty and suffering. For so many centuries these proudest of people were subjected to unspeakable hardships and humiliation at the hands of foreigners, and though they have started anew they must surely doubt that anyone who has not shared in their history can ever really understand the tremendous and complex human struggles that they face in building a wholly new kind of civilization. Just as no friend, however close, can ever share the countless common memories that unite a family, so hardly any foreigner, however long he lives in China, however affectionate his relationships, ever manages to step inside the magic circle.

3 The Celestial City

In Peking I always feel as if I'm living in two dimensions of time. Here, more than in any other city in the world, I feel the past rubbing shoulders with the present and both jostle me for attention. China is a nation bursting with new ideas, new buildings, new factories, new experiments, new education, new medicine — a country whose people are establishing wholly new relationships with one another. And Peking is the very heart and core of it. There's a lot of accumulated débris from the past and the Chinese are pushing it aside — old concepts and feudal customs that have been handed down from long ago, absurd conventions and rigid rules of behaviour that for centuries have held the Chinese in a kind of mental bondage. They are right: all this has to go, though that is easier said than done.

With all this new activity, Peking strikes me as being the youngest city in the world; but having said that, I know it is, in fact, one of the oldest. The past is still here, influencing the day-to-day lives of the people in a thousand different ways. Their behaviour to each other and to strangers, their respect for the old, their script and language, the subtle nuances of their poetry, their delight in the play of words and meanings, their humour, their rough and often bawdy colloquial speech, their ingrained resistance to anything foreign and their stubborn certainty that they are always right — all this is part of their cultural heritage and it's all still here.

Late one afternoon I was standing at the intersection of Tai Ji Chang and Changan (a boulevard much wider than the Champs Élysées) that runs from east to west across Peking. It was the rush hour. The air was full of the tooting of cars and trucks. Five, six, seven crowded trolley-buses were waiting in line for the traffic lights to change. Across Changan from where I stood was the newest hotel in Peking, seventeen storeys high, more modern, a businessman told me, more comfortable than any hotel he'd been to in New York, London or Paris. Perhaps in fifteen years, I thought (or sooner, for things move fast here) Peking may become just another huge modern metropolis.

26

Newspaper delivery in the *hutungs*.

Taking a morning ride.

Hutungs bathed in morning light.

Practising the flute by the
Forbidden City wall—before
going to work.

In a Peking restaurant.

Preparing the celebrated
Peking duck.

Slices of water
melon being sold in
the streets.

But then again it probably will not. Peking will be modernized, yes; but it will never become a London or a New York, an unorganized, unplanned jungle of competing interests, for the people here have an altogether different vision of their future and it will never be wholly severed from the past.

I strolled west along Changan. There in the distance, as if echoing my thoughts, was Tian An Men, the Gate of Heavenly Peace, with its curved roof outlined against the evening light. Massive, serene, marvellously proportioned, standing guard as it has for centuries at the entrance to the Imperial City. At that moment it symbolized for me the enormous momentum and continuity of China's ancient civilization.

There was still time before the light faded, so with these musings still in my mind I walked to Tian An Men. Standing before this towering structure, I looked up to near where the rafters touch the wall. There, red against a blue background, was the five-starred symbol of revolutionary China – so here again, the old and the new. Again, that odd sensation of living in a city that is both the newest and the oldest in the world. With some extraordinary power of alchemy, the people of Peking are combining what is best in their ancient culture with the most dynamic and most advanced of social revolutions.

This intermingling of history with a new vision of what human societies might become is what makes Peking, for me, the most fascinating city in the world. Thus, if one is to understand today's Peking it is necessary to know something of its past.

The best place to start when unravelling Peking's long and turbulent history is Tian An Men. It was from here that imperial edicts and proclamations were issued. The scrolls on which the emperor's 'divine decrees' were written would be flung from the high parapet to officials kneeling humbly below, whose duty it was to disseminate them across the empire. Today for the Chinese, Tian An Men has an even greater significance. It was from the same parapet used by the emperors that at three o'clock in the afternoon on October 1st, 1949, Mao Tsetung proclaimed to nearly half a million people crowded in the square below him the establishment of the People's Republic of China. Since that day Tian An Men has become the central symbol of the new China. It is depicted on coins and stamps and there can scarcely be a home in this entire nation of 900 million people that does not have, pinned on the wall or propped over a fireplace, a coloured photograph of this ancient and beautiful structure. The dream of every Chinese child, however far away he may live, is to travel to Peking and see Tian An Men and perhaps be photographed in front of it to show his people back home.

Before going through the high arched entrance of Tian An Men, let us spend a little time in the great 38-hectare square that represents the new China. Widened and repaved in 1959, it is now the largest square in any city in the world – five times larger than the Red Square in Moscow, large enough to hold a million people. The square is flanked by two great buildings, both half a kilometre long: the Museum of Chinese History on the east side, and the Great Hall of the People on the west. In the centre of the square is a simple granite column that rises forty-five metres from a white marble platform, the Memorial to the People's Heroes. In 1977 between this column and Cheng Yang Men – another gate just north of Chienmen (the great southern gate that once divided the outer and inner city), an immensely impressive memorial hall to Mao Tsetung was constructed and completed in just six months.

The Great Hall of the People to the west is even larger inside than its appearance would suggest. Within it is an auditorium that can seat 10,000 and a banqueting hall in which 5,000 people can dine at 500 circular tables without in any way feeling crowded. I have attended many splendid banquets given to visiting dignatories or heads of state, and it always astonishes me how the attendants are able to serve so many people so many dishes (and always piping hot) without delay and without the slightest clatter or fuss. A miracle of organization. To the diplomatic corps in Peking and the foreign correspondents who must go frequently to these official banquets, they may become routine and unexciting, and perhaps to the Chinese officials too. To the distinguished visitor, seated with almost all the highest-ranking leaders of the government on each side and with a band playing music of his country, such a banquet must be among the most memorable experiences of his visit to Peking.

The auditorium on the ground floor is impressive in the simplicity of its design and the daring of its engineering – the first gallery spans the entire width of the hall without a single supporting column. The hall is used for meetings of the National People's Congress – the largest legislative assembly in the world – and other important meetings; but I have attended concerts and dramatic performances there as well. I found it a moving experience to sit in an audience of 10,000 ordinary Chinese people – factory workers, soldiers, office workers – dressed in their everyday clothes listening with rapt attention to the Peking Symphony Orchestra or watching one of the great dance-dramas that they stage with such amazing colour and effect.

With an auditorium of this enormous size there is usually a problem

Cheng Yang Men, newly re-decorated, stands between Chienmen and the Mao Tsetung Memorial Hall.

of audibility. The Chinese designers solved this in an ingenious manner. Set in the back of each seat is a minute loudspeaker, so small that even with one's ear close to it the sound is barely audible. Yet collectively, these 10,000 loudspeakers allow the voice of even the quietest speaker to be heard throughout the hall. When this vast complex of the Great Hall was being constructed, the people of Peking – even children – were asked to lend a hand. They came in thousands in their spare time and at week-ends to help the construction engineers.

The Great Hall of the People, the Historical Museum on the other side of the square, and other large buildings in Peking – ten in all – were built in 1959, and completed in ten months, a fact only believable to those who have themselves watched the speed of construction here. *Ten* large buildings, built in *ten* months, to celebrate the *tenth* anniversary of the founding of the People's Republic. (The Chinese delight in arranging felicitous conjunctions of numbers.)

These buildings, the immense square and the more recently constructed Mao Tsetung Memorial Hall, represent the new Peking.

Walking across the white marble bridge and through the deeply set entrance of Tian An Men, one enters the grounds of the Imperial Palace and steps back into history. The sounds of traffic, the sense of modern movement and activity are quite stilled. Walking along a tree-lined avenue, through another stately gate, Duan Men, one sees ahead Wu Men, the Meridian Gate, the entrance to the Forbidden City itself.

29

Here, within the holy of holies, feudal emperors isolated themselves in the midst of unimaginable pomp and luxury, surrounded by thousands of concubines and eunuchs.

The Forbidden City is no longer, of course, forbidden. Here, walking towards Wu Men one sees fathers and mothers out for a stroll with their children, soldiers on leave, workers, peasants with white kerchiefs round their foreheads, tourists with cameras, members of China's minority nationalists in their colourful costumes; an atmosphere altogether like a free-and-easy Sunday afternoon. This entrance to the Forbidden City is immensely impressive. Standing in front of the towering dull-red, fortress-like walls of Wu Men, one can very easily picture the emperors of old on the parapet gazing down on the troops of the Imperial Guard below.

Within the 100 hectares of the Forbidden City there are courtyards of every size and nature – some extensive enough for 10,000 troops or courtiers to be assembled before the emperor; while others are quite small – intimate enclosures with perhaps a lotus pond or a strange-shaped rock surrounded by peonies. Near the main palaces there are figures of birds, tortoises, dragons, huge bronze urns that were formerly plated in gold. There are halls that are veritable treasure houses of art – exquisite porcelains, brocades, scrolls, golden artefacts, jade and ivory, the creation of thousands of worker-artists of the past.

Days, months, can be spent wandering through buildings with romantic names: the Palace of Heavenly Purity, the Palace of Earthly Tranquillity, the Pavilion of Depth of Knowledge, the Tower of Propitious Clouds, the Caves of the House of Fairies, the Pavilion of the Floating Jade, the Palace of Peace in Old Age, the Pavilion of the Purest Perfumes ... the list is almost endless.

Dominating this diversity and giving a sense of harmony and unparalleled dignity and magnificence are six great halls, one following the other, all set facing south along the central north–south axis. Indeed, from Tian An Men the south entrance to Shen Wu Men, the great gate in the north wall, all the main gates, halls and palaces are set on this same north–south axis.

Passing through Wu Men one is confronted by perhaps the most perfect of the great courtyards. Through it there winds the Golden Water River, curved like a bow and crossed by five white marble bridges. And from here across this courtyard one can see the next gateway, the Gate of Great Harmony, guarded by two immense bronze lions.

Passing through the Gate of Great Harmony, looking north across the largest court of all, one sees the most important of all the buildings

The Great Hall of the People: *top*, the banqueting hall, and *centre*, the auditorium.

Looking across Tian An Men Square to the Great Hall.

The Mao Tsetung Memorial Hall.

in the Forbidden City – the Hall of Supreme Harmony. Over sixty metres wide and thirty deep, the Hall is set on a wide marble terrace and is approached by three flights of marble stairs. This is the innermost sanctum, called by the ancient Chinese 'The Centre of the World'. Step inside the hall and there in the subdued light, raised on a richly decorated platform, is the Dragon Throne, the seat of the emperor himself. The entire hall is lacquered and the throne is surrounded with urns, incense burners, carved dragons, figures of elephants and monsters – anything that would create an air of mystery, awe and majesty. The ceiling, almost thirty metres high, is supported by magnificent round pillars, some vermilion-red, some in decorated gilt, and high up in the centre of the ceiling, is a great gilded dragon. On either side of the throne stand two cranes, their heads turned towards the throne, their grace and simplicity standing out in contrast to their ornate surroundings. In years past, the dim light, the smoke and scent of incense, the rhythmic beating of a distant gong, the glimmer of gilt and lacquer, the great pillars, the yellow-carpeted steps leading to the throne – everything was calculated to fill with fear those who came into the presence of the emperor. Officials trembled as they knelt before him to receive his orders; envoys bringing tribute were required to kneel and kowtow their heads to the floor nine times. For here before them, in robes of silk and gold, sat the very Son of Heaven. His word was supreme. With a gesture he could, and often did, order a man to be beheaded for the most trivial mistake, and on his word alone 100,000 men could be sent into battle.

When did it all begin?

China's two earliest dynasties were the Xia and the Shang, between the 21st and 11th centuries B.C. Before that the riddles remain insoluble, with legend, fantasy and reality all mixed up in the mists of time. As for Peking, historians believe it was first built as a small garrison town to guard the fertile plains of northern China against marauding tribes. It was not until 720 B.C. that the city emerged from obscurity to become a capital for the first time – not yet of a united China but of the fief state of Yan.

We cannot trace here all that has happened to Peking between then and now, but what an extraordinary story it is! Since that time 2,700 years ago, this city has experienced all manner of vicissitudes, mutations, periods of great glory and cataclysmic disasters. It has changed its name at least eight times. It has been sacked, demolished by earthquakes, occupied by foreign troops, totally destroyed, overrun by bandits, hopelessly misruled, and more than once its people have suffered the most ruthless massacre, torture, pillage and rape. Even in the last 800 years Peking has been rebuilt four times. Yet, Peking, and this is surely one of the mysteries of history, survived every disaster always, like the phoenix, rising again, more magnificent than before.

During the Chou dynasty (1031–221 B.C.) the name of Peking was Chi. After 475 B.C. came the period known as the 'Period of Warring States'. This was a time when literature and the arts flourished, when great scholars and philosophers emerged – among them K'ung Fu-tzu, better known by his Latin name of Confucius. It also heralded the beginning of China's feudal age. The series of internecine wars continued for two and a half centuries, until 221 B.C. when the Chou were finally overthrown and the state of Ch'in emerged supreme. The Ch'in occupied territory in Shensi Province in north-west China. By learning the art of fighting on horseback from barbarian tribes in the north, they gained sufficient military strength to overrun more cultured states that still relied on cumbersome chariots. Eventually they conquered and unified all China for the first time. Their leader, on founding the Ch'in dynasty, chose the title Shi Huang Di, meaning First Sovereign Emperor. His dynasty is now regarded as being the first imperial dynasty. And it was from the dynastic name of the Ch'in that the word China was derived.

The reign of Shi Huang Di radically changed and charted the course of Chinese history for the next 2,000 years. Under his rule, the old feudal system was consolidated and a system of national administration through provincial governors was established that was to be retained almost until the present day. The written language, weights and measures, and even the gauge of wheeled vehicles, were standardized. Highways were constructed to link all parts of the country. And since his unified nation-state needed to strengthen her outer defences and clearly define the boundaries between the Chinese world of civilization and the outside world of barbarism, Shi Huang Di ordered that old sections of defensive walls should be repaired and linked together. The result was the completion of the most massive construction project ever undertaken by man: the Great Wall of China. When finally connected, the wall of the north frontier combined to cover the equivalent of nearly one-tenth of the world's circumference. Punctuated with 30,000 towers, it stretched from the sea at Shanhai Guan, westwards north of Peking and then south-west across Shanshi to the Yellow River, finally ending west of Suchow near the Gobi Desert. From end to end, the world's longest wall extended more than 3,000 kilometres, and with its meanderings and loops the full extent of the structure measured nearly 6,000 kilometres.

Today foreign visitors to Peking will usually take the one-hour drive north on an excursion to see the section of the Great Wall at Petaling beyond the Nankow Pass. It is a remarkable sight. The wall is seven metres thick at the base and up to nine metres high. Viewed from the battlements, it winds into the distance like an immense dragon whose head and tail are invisible. On its course from sea to desert it dips into great passes, rises thousands of metres up mountain-sides, and for the most part is wide enough to allow five horsemen to ride abreast. Of a million conscripted labourers who built this immense wall, it is said that only half survived.

The various sieges, captures and name-changes that Peking endured over the next 3,000 years are too numerous to catalogue here. Dynasties rose and fell. China fragmented again into conflicting states and became united again. While the masses suffered under brutally autocratic rule, China's ruling classes enjoyed the fruits of dramatic advances in the arts and sciences. By the 1130s A.D., during the Sung dynasty, a new power calling themselves the Chin (meaning 'golden') had arisen from the tribes in the north. They took Peking by force, named it Zhong Jing (Central Capital), and there created a city modelled on Kaifeng, the capital of the Sung emperor in the south, though on a smaller scale. It was said that to build the Zhong Jing palaces 800,000 labourers and 400,000 soldiers were employed. Yet the city could not even remotely compare with the magnificence of Kaifeng in the south. For the vast majority of Chinese, life was an experience of unrelieved toil and poverty. For the leisured classes, the Sung period in the south and the Chin in the north reached a height of culture and sophistication never before equalled in history. Today we still stand in awe before the refinement and restraint of their painting and poetry, the delicacy of their porcelains, the beauty of their fabrics. Their philosophy reflects an exquisite appreciation of the most subtle and universal relations of life and an almost total disregard of the teeming and often hungry masses outside the palace walls.

Beyond the Great Wall, however, was another fast-growing power, one lacking the kind of culture and artistic refinement that was flourishing in China, and yet far ahead in military strength. The armies of the mighty Genghis Khan were about to invade. And these nomadic Mongols had no interest in grabbing land for land's sake. Their sole aims were loot – and the pleasure they derived from destruction. As Genghis Khan bluntly expressed it: 'A man's greatest joy is to defeat his

The Great Wall along its
6,000-kilometre journey.

The Temple of Heaven.

enemies, to pursue them, to take from them that which they possessed, to see their families in tears, to ride their horses and possess their wives and daughters.'

Held up at the Great Wall by the Chin troops, both armies fought with the greatest ferocity. At last, like water bursting through a broken dam, the Mongol armies, though outnumbered four to one, swept down upon Peking. The Chin emperor, who was buying time to flee south, stalled the Great Khan by offering him gifts. When Genghis came again in May 1215, vast quantities of gold, jewelry, 1,000 young men and girls and 3,000 horses were handed over in a second, more grotesque, attempt at appeasement. But this time it didn't work and the Emperor fled. The Hordes* had cohesion and discipline and far superior horsemanship, with every man a trained archer able to shoot from the saddle at full gallop. Now, with the city demoralized by the emperor's departure, there was no halting the wave of terror and destruction. The carnage went on for weeks. Thousands of defenceless people were mercilessly butchered, the women raped, the palaces looted and destroyed and whatever remained was set on fire. When the last of the Khan's army finally withdrew, there was scarcely a house standing among the desolate and smoking ruins. It was one of the cataclysmic events in history. A city representing the most advanced culture in the world had been destroyed by a nomadic savage who had no thought but to kill, pillage and burn. No one at that moment of frenzied destruction could have dreamed that forty years later under Kublai Khan, the grandson of the very man who had destroyed it, Peking would be rebuilt on an even more magnificent scale. Genghis Khan was the supreme nomad. He did not build. He moved his armies across vast areas of Asia and into Europe, feeding on the wealth and labour of others.

His grandson knew that a lasting civilization could be achieved only by a settled community. Though ruling an immense empire that stretched from the China Sea to the banks of the Dneiper and from the Himalayas to the Arctic Circle, Kublai Khan, astonishingly, chose the relatively small city of Peking as his winter capital.

'In Xanadu,' wrote Coleridge, 'did Kublai Khan a stately pleasure dome decree.' In Peking, which he named Ta-Tu (Great Capital),†

---

*The word 'Hordes' does not indicate great numbers. It is derived from the word *ordu* meaning 'camp'. Repeatedly the words 'Mongol hordes' have been used incorrectly, giving the impression that Genghis Khan's armies were of immense size.

† Ta-Tu was the Han Chinese name for Peking. The Mongol name was 'Khanbalik' and it was by this name that Peking was known by Marco Polo.

Kublai decreed much more. He ordered that Peking was to be the grandest city known to man, for: 'If the palaces and metropolitan adornments are not beautiful and imposing, they will not be able to command the respect of the Empire.' Though still smaller and less opulent than some of the cities in the south, never before had any city been built with such disregard for cost. A complex of palaces, court-yards, lakes, gardens and artificial hills – everything that would add lustre to the emperor was included. The following year Kublai pro-claimed the beginning of a new Chinese dynasty entitled Da Yuan (meaning Great Origin) with himself as the first emperor. Then, as the self-made Son of Heaven, he proceeded to become like the Han Chin-ese in everything but his ethnic origin, respecting the customs of the Hans, adopting their method of government and their style of living.

The Peking of the Mongols was built as a square, surrounded by walls nine kilometres long in all. The main palace was built behind an inner square of walls guarded by fortified towers. Twelve thousand mounted knights made up the Great Khan's personal guard and 3,000 were permanently on duty at the central palace. It was from here that Kublai, with his Han Chinese advisers, administered his immense empire.

Here also he held feasts of *Arabian Nights'* splendour in a banqueting hall that could seat 6,000 guests, and here, on New Year's Day, his 5,000 elephants were paraded in stately procession together with a huge herd of camels.

The world knew very little about China then. Occasionally, from Arab traders, word would come filtering back of a fabulous city in the Far East. But the descriptions were fragmentary and were considered to be legend. It was Marco Polo, a young Venetian traveller, who brought back to an astonished and only half-believing Europe the first coherent account of this far-off civilization. Marco Polo visited Peking in 1275 when he was seventeen. He became an employee of Kublai Khan and remained in Peking until 1292. But the city that Marco Polo attempted to describe, 'the greatest and most wonderful that was ever seen', with palaces standing on marble bases and halls all covered with gold and silver and blue, was not destined to last. The pride of Kublai Khan survived no longer than the Mongol rule of China – just one hundred years.

Kublai's successors were, like the former emperors, unconcerned with the abject poverty of the peasants, who were already reduced to starvation level by a series of floods and other natural disasters. The rulers hastened the inevitable civil war by imposing the most crippling taxes to maintain the fantastic luxuries of the Peking court. Resentment by the peasants against the non-Han Mongol rulers became widespread and merely awaited a leader to flare into open revolt.

Chu, the son of a poor peasant in Anhwei Province, ever since he was eighteen had been gathering popular support for an onslaught against the Mongols. In 1386 he led an army of peasants against Peking. The city capitulated without much struggle and Chu proclaimed the beginning of the Ming (meaning 'brilliant') dynasty. After a century of what was then considered foreign rule China once more had a native Han emperor.

But this did not do much to alter the life of the common people. The centuries-old system of a ruling élite was so firmly entrenched that peasant uprisings never resulted in improved conditions for the people. The triumphant rebels merely formed the new élite, no less tyrannical than those they had overthrown. The ex-peasant Chu, as the first Ming emperor, took for his 'reign title' the name of Hung Wu.

Basically the Mongols during their century of power had changed nothing. Under the third Ming emperor, Chu's son Yung-lo, Peking was for the last time dismantled – not by armies and destruction but by thousands upon thousands of builders, labourers and craftsmen. The city was dismantled and rebuilt so thoroughly that very little of the Mongol capital remained. It is this city, built by Yung-lo and completed in 1421 which we see in Peking today – the Imperial City and the Forbidden City within it, the Temple of Heaven, the palaces and the great city gates. In all, over 700 buildings were erected by Yung-lo and most of these still exist. For the first time in its history the city was known by its present name Peking (meaning Northern Capital).

Yung-lo liked to do things on a grand scale. He commissioned the largest encyclopaedia ever compiled – the Yung-lo Da Dian comprising over 11,000 manuscript volumes. He was the emperor who sent Admiral Zheng He on seven great voyages of discovery. Some sixty years before Columbus began his voyage to the New World with three modest-sized vessels and about a hundred men, Zheng was commanding a fleet with some 20,000 men that sailed to India, to the South Seas, and as far as the East African coasts. But Yung-lo, contrary to his name, meaning 'perpetual happiness', was a despot like so many of the Ming emperors who came after him. The rebuilding of Peking, the commissioning of works of arts, the dispatching of his fleet to bring back such curiosities as ostriches and giraffes – were for self-glorification and not at all for the benefit of the people. This was also true of Emperor Wan-li, a pampered child of nine who came to the throne in 1581. His reign lasted over forty years, the longest of any Ming emperor. It was a period renowned for its cultural brilliance. But the ruler himself contributed nothing to this brilliance; always self-indulgent, he absorbed himself in a world of private extravagance. He was totally cut off from his subjects, isolated in a court that comprised 9,000 palace women and 70,000 eunuchs.

Wan-li built himself a large mausoleum which is reached by the Great Spirit Way – an extraordinary avenue lined with massive sculptures of warriors, elephants, camels, lions and unicorns. There, in a beautiful valley below the Tien Shou Shan hills, are the tombs of thirteen Ming emperors. The tomb that Wan-li built for himself consists of five great halls. A notice posted near the stone staircase leading down to the tomb tells us that it was built at a cost of a million gold bars and '65 million manpowers' – enough manpower, it explains, to have produced sufficient grain to feed one million people for six years.

By the time the last of the sixteen Ming emperors, Cheng Zhen, came to power in 1627, the Ming dynasty was already doomed. After so many years of extravagance and misgovernment, the country was in general disorder, threatened by revolution within and foreign invasion from without.

Li Zi-cheng, one of the greatest leaders of peasant rebellions in Chinese history, had begun organizing the peasants. In eighteen years his peasant army swept over many provinces in north China and actually took the capital, Peking. But, as happened so frequently in such peasant rebellions, after winning a victory some leaders became corrupt, discipline became lax; some, through personal jealousy and ambition, went over to the enemy. Thus the Ming army commander, Wu San-gui, opened the way for the Manchu troops to enter north China, the peasant rebellion was defeated and the city of Peking was taken by the Manchus. The last Ming emperor, having slain his family with his own sword, hanged himself from a locust tree on Coal Hill which overlooked his beloved Forbidden City. Having captured Peking, the Manchu kept it for themselves, making it their capital and expanding their control and authority throughout the empire. For their dynasty they took the name of Ching (meaning 'pure'). They were to rule China for the next 250 years.

Under the old Ming regime, the entry into China of any foreigners had been forbidden, nor could any Chinese leave the country. The most important breakthrough came during Wan-li's reign in 1582, when the Jesuit Matteo Ricci arrived in China from Europe. Foreign traders could only deal, under government supervision, at designated trading posts along the frontiers. But Ricci came as a missionary and a scholar and was allowed to set up the first mission in China, though it was nineteen years before he was permitted to visit Peking. (The Peking observatory was set up with the help of the Jesuits.)

Ricci was essentially an exception to the rule. China's curtain of isolation from the rest of the world continued in the Ching (Manchu) dynasty and on into modern times. There is no better example of the Chinese suspicion of foreigners (fully justified as later history was to prove) than their response to George III's suggestion that stronger trade links between Britain and China should be established, and that ambassadors should be exchanged in London and Peking. Lord George Macartney, the British diplomat, was sent out in 1793 as ambassador to make the necessary overtures. He sailed with a great retinue and all manner of gifts intended for the elderly Emperor, Ch'ien Lung – a planetarium, a hot-air balloon, scientific instruments, an assortment of clocks and watches.

Macartney and his aides were royally entertained by the 82-year-old Emperor. 'I have seen "King Solomon" in all his glory,' Macartney wrote in his diary after attending a five-hour banquet with non-stop distractions – wrestling, acrobatics, wire-dancing, play-acting and a fireworks display. Yet his mission accomplished absolutely nothing towards establishing an embassy in Peking. George III's requests were never properly discussed. After weeks of inactivity, Macartney at last received in his quarters a procession of servants who ceremoniously transported a yellow silk armchair. On the chair lay the Emperor's written reply to George III. It was in the form of an edict:

As to what you have requested in your message, O King,
namely to be allowed to send one of your subjects to
reside in the Celestial Empire to look after your country's
trade this ... definitely cannot be done ...
  We have never valued ingenious articles, nor do we have
the slightest need of your country's manufactures ...
  You, O King, should simply act in conformity with our
wishes by strengthening your loyalty and swearing
perpetual obedience so as to ensure that your country
may share the blessings of peace.

In simple truth, China at that time had no need of trade with foreigners. Britain, on the other hand, had developed an insatiable taste for Chinese tea. Old Ch'ien Lung had, however, overlooked one item when he told George III that China needed none of England's manufactures, and it was the British who discovered the one commodity that the

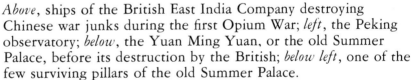

Above, ships of the British East India Company destroying Chinese war junks during the first Opium War; *left*, the Peking observatory; *below*, the Yuan Ming Yuan, or the old Summer Palace, before its destruction by the British; *below left*, one of the few surviving pillars of the old Summer Palace.

Chinese found irresistible – opium. Traffic in opium had been declared illegal by the Chinese government in the late eighteenth century, but this was not enforced until 1837. By then it was too late. The East India Company had thousands of hectares under opium. The export of opium was good for British commerce and good for British shipping. The illegal and subversive drug was being smuggled into China at the rate of 40,000 chests a year. It was estimated that this trade had created two million addicts, the majority drawn from the upper classes – many of them officials who could easily be corrupted by the drug. The moral and social dangers were serious enough; what equally alarmed imperial Peking were the economic implications. For the first time in China's history the value of her imports exceeded that of her exports, and precious silver was flowing out of the country in such huge quantities that raging inflation was imminent. The situation was explosive and finally the fuse was lit when an imperial commissioner from Peking seized and destroyed 20,000 chests of opium belonging to British merchants in Canton. It gave Britain the false excuse for the first 'Opium War', which was ended in 1842 by the cynically unjust Treaty of Nanking. China was compelled by the peace terms to cede to Britain the island of Hong Kong and to pay an indemnity of £100 million for a war she had never sought. The peace treaty did not mention opium.

Exploited and oppressed by foreigners and by their own upper class, the people of China rose in rebellion. During the ten years after the Opium War there were more than a hundred peasant uprisings. The Ching rulers suppressed these rebellions by force of arms. Yet these numerous uprisings were but the forerunners of the Taiping Revolution that was to shake the Ching dynasty to its foundations.

China's self-imposed isolation from the outside world was ultimately self-defeating. It kept her ignorant of modern weapons so that foreign powers had no difficulty in taking by force of arms that which they were unable to obtain by diplomacy and China had to submit for a century and a half to alien exploitation. In 1858 a second, equally unjustifiable, 'Opium War' ended in a treaty that gave Britain further trade advantages, an indemnity of £20 million, and – most alarming to the emperor personally – the right to conduct diplomatic relations 'on terms of equality' and to have a British minister resident in Peking. Two years later, in order to force the ratification of this treaty, the British and French governments ordered their expeditionary forces to march on Peking. Again the old capital was to be pillaged by foreign invaders.

Thirty kilometres north-west of Peking the French troops came upon the Yuan Ming Yuan ('Round Bright Garden'), a vast complex of scarlet

Inside one of Peking's department
stores.

'Times have changed. Men and women
are now equal. Criticize the idea that
men are superior to women.'

Above, Wu Men: gateway to the Forbidden City.
Facing page, Tian An Men: gateway to the Imperial City; and looking through, towards the Imperial City.

Carefully restoring the decoration on the ancient buildings.

Aspects of the Forbidden City: *above* and *left*, courtyards, and *below*, detail of the rafters, showing the symbol of the Chinese People's Republic.

and gold halls, gardens, lakes and pavilions that was built in 1709 as an imperial residence and subsequently used as a Summer Palace where the grand councillors of the emperor had special apartments. Arriving there, the French troops went into a frenzy of looting and took off everything they could carry. A week later, in reprisal for the killing of two British envoys, British troops acting under the orders of Lord Elgin went one better. They razed the magnificent buildings – over 200 pavilions, halls and temples – to the ground. 'You can scarcely imagine,' one British soldier wrote home, 'the beauty and magnificence of the places we burnt.'

A few ruins of the Yuan Ming Yuan still remain. Where the old Summer Palace once stood – at one time possibly among the most beautiful array of buildings in all China – are a few marble pillars standing stark and gaunt against the sky. By walking over the ground one is able to trace the area where some of the buildings had stood and discover broken plinths and decorated archways that are now half-covered by grass and shrubs. It is a strange experience to see these remnants of beauty – so wantonly destroyed. Not this time by savage Mongol Hordes as in the past but by Europeans, and not long ago.

Later another Summer Palace was built, and it remains a lasting monument to the absurd extravagances of the most remarkable and terrible woman in the history of imperial China. Her name was Yehonala and she entered the Forbidden City in 1852 as a sixteen-year-old concubine.*

At the time of Tzu Hsi's arrival at the Forbidden City the Ching (Manchu) dynasty was being threatened by another growing rebellion in the south. There a young peasant, Hong Xiu, had proclaimed himself the Heavenly King of the Heavenly Kingdom of the Great Peace. His movement had a strong element of Christianity. To the sophisticated at the Peking court a movement under this dubious leadership must at first have appeared as nothing to be much concerned about. Yet Hong, wandering through the countryside as a pedlar, was making thousands of converts. His appeal was to the poor and dispossessed; to the peasants without land, to the hungry and homeless and to all those who were most looked down upon in the rigid Confucian society. All property, he said, was to be publicly owned and land was to be divided equally among all, including women. Money was to be held in a public treasury and used for the sick, widows and orphans. His vision was a

*Yehonala was born Lan Kuei ('Little Orchid') but is usually referred to as Tzu Hsi, the name she was known by after she gained power.

society based on the brotherhood of man. Thousands flocked to his standard as he set out to challenge and overthrow the Manchu dynasty in Peking. The resulting uprising, known as the Taiping Rebellion, was destined to last thirteen years and before it was finally crushed with the help of foreign arms and foreign military leadership it was to cause the most appalling suffering.*

The extent of the destruction caused during these thirteen years of the Taiping Rebellion was appalling. The courage and tenacity of the peasants is a measure of how deep was their sense of oppression and their resentment of foreign intervention. Six hundred walled cities had been occupied, five provinces were turned into a wilderness as the armies fought back and forth across them. Before the end, more than 20 million people had perished. No conflict in human history had previously caused such destruction or so great a loss of life, nor was it to happen again until the great wars in our present century.

During the years when the imperial armies were fighting to subdue the Taiping rebels, Tzu Hsi who, as we have seen, had entered the Forbidden City as a teenage concubine, had moved into a commanding position of authority. Five years after her arrival she provided the ailing Emperor with his only son, and this consolidated her power. At the Emeror's death this child was declared his successor and his mother, as Empress Dowager, became Regent. This woman, having now assumed absolute power, clung to it by cunning and manipulation until her death in 1908, forty-seven years later.†

It is difficult to separate fact from fiction when it comes to this last all-powerful ruler of the Imperial Chinese Empire. Stories of her private life of debauchery are legion, and mostly impossible to substantiate. As for her public life, that was one long display of pomp and ceremony, the most appalling waste and cruelty.

In 1875, on the death of her emperor son, she engineered that her nephew, a sickly child of three, should be placed on the throne, thus managing again to keep the reins of supreme power in her own hands. The Kuang-hsu Emperor, as he was called, 'the Emperor of Glorious Succession', was of poor physique and was chronically ill. From the time that he was brought to the Forbidden City to become emperor he lived

---

* It was a British general, Charles George Gordon (whose death in Khartoum in 1885 became a celebrated event in British history), who was placed in command of the Chinese imperial troops that put down the Taiping Rebellion.
† I am greatly indebted for much of my information about Tzu Hsi to Marina Warner's excellent book, *The Dragon Empress* (Weidenfeld, 1972).

a lonely and isolated life, neglected even by his servants. Even as an adult, when he could legally have exercised his authority as emperor, the Empress Dowager kept him under strict control. At the age of twenty-six, after China had been disastrously defeated in a war with Japan, he associated himself with a movement urging the modernizing of Chinese society, which aimed (without his knowledge) at the over-throw of the Empress Dowager. This plan was discovered by the Dowager. She ordered her guards to seize the Emperor and she had him taken as a prisoner to one of the islands in the Summer Palace lake. Fourteen of Kuang-hsu's eunuchs were executed and in the Emperor's name she announced his virtual abdication.

The one joy in Kuang-hsu's forlorn life was a pretty and lively girl, the Pearl Concubine, of whom he was genuinely fond, and perhaps she was of him. The Empress Dowager, intensely jealous of her, saw to it that she was prevented from joining Kuang-hsu on his island prison.

In 1888, at a time of economic crisis, the Empress Dowager insisted on squandering enormous sums of money on building the Summer Palace to replace the one destroyed by the British in 1860. Being a lover of water picnics she ordered that the many new buildings should include an ostentatious palace erected beside an artificial lake and a marble pavilion rising from the water in the shape of a Mississippi paddle-steamer. As always, she was indulging her own fancies with total disregard of national security, for the money she deviously provided for her Summer Palace had originally been allocated for the urgent moder-nization of the antiquated Chinese navy. Her neglected Chinese navy was destroyed by a modernized Japanese fleet. Her marble paddle-steamer is still there today.

The Emperor of Japan had recognized the need for reform but the woman behind the Manchu Dragon throne resisted change with a stubbornness matched only by her vanity and greed. She is remem-bered above all for her tenacity and fanaticism in resisting 'Western barbarism', a determination that dominated her entire thinking.

It is hardly surprising, therefore, that after some initial vacillation she should have sympathized with a group of fanatics whose original objec-tive was to eliminate the Manchus and restore the Ming dynasty. The Manchu court turned the rebellion into an anti-foreign movement. These fanatics were known as the Boxers and they launched a violent campaign against Western missionaries and their Chinese converts. By May 1900, the Boxers were at the gates of Peking; by the end of June almost every foreign building in the capital, with the exception of the legations had been burned to the ground. That month the chancellor of the Japanese legation was murdered. A few days later the German minister, Baron von Ketteler, was fatally shot while making a short journey by sedan chair in Peking. The siege of the European legations swiftly followed. 'The foreigners are like fish in the stew pan,' wrote the Empress Dowager. During the fighting, in the hope that the flames would reach the legation buildings where the foreigners were besieged, the Boxers set fire to the oldest library in the world, the Hanlin Yuan, and thousands of priceless documents recording the history and philosophy of China from ancient times were uselessly destroyed.

The Western powers mounted an army consisting of troops from Japan, Russia, the United States, Britain and France, to march on Peking to rescue the surrounded foreigners. As the relief forces neared Peking, the court within the Forbidden City was thrown into confusion. The Empress Dowager frantically called meeting after meeting of her advisers. In a rage of frustration she ordered three ministers to be executed. She issued wild and conflicting edicts which only further demoralized her supporters.

On August 14th the first troops of the relieving army crept through the water gate under the city wall. The next day Peking fell. At daybreak that day, Tzu Hsi ordered the sickly Emperor and his wife to come to her quarters. She stripped them and herself of all jewelry and fine clothes. She cut her fifteen-centimetre finger nails, dressed herself in the coarse blue clothes of the peasants and threw a peasant scarf over her head. As she, with her nephew, the Emperor and his wife, were about to climb into the wooden carts which were to bear them away, the pretty Pearl Concubine threw herself on her knees at the feet of the Empress Dowager imploring her not to flee and thus bring everlasting dishonour to the dynasty. In a fury, the Empress Dowager ordered her eunuchs to throw the Pearl Concubine into a well and drown her, and this was done before the very eyes of the Emperor who loved her. Then the northern gate of the Forbidden City (the Gate of Spiritual Valour) was opened and in their disguise the Empress Dowager with the Emperor and Empress of China escaped from Peking and made their way to Sian, 1,100 kilometres away. There, in the former capital of the Tang dynasty, the Dowager once again was able to live in luxury.

While she was gone from Peking, representatives of the Western powers discussed how best to punish the Chinese for the destruction they had caused. It was decided that China should pay a large money indemnity and should allow foreigners resident in China still greater privileges and influences. These matters having been settled, the Western powers decided that it would be more convenient to deal directly

46

Right, The Empress Dowager;
below, her counsellors during
the Boxer Rebellion.

After the threats to the Dowager's regime, the Chinese army was 'modernized'. This photograph shows the first arsenal, built at Nanking.

with the Empress Dowager than through her viceroys, and she was invited back to Peking.

She took her time. Hundreds of pack animals and carts carried the possessions she had accumulated during her exile. At Kaifeng she spent several weeks resting and enjoying sight-seeing trips to monuments and temples. Having consulted her astrologers as to the day for her return, she was informed that 2 p.m. on January 7th, 1902 would be the propitious moment. The last part of her journey was on the newly built British railway – it was her first journey by train. It required four freight trains to carry her luggage; her own train was fitted with a throne and was upholstered in yellow damask.

When the train arrived at Peking station, not far from Chienmen near the main gate between the Outer and Inner City, she entered a richly decorated covered chair. Reaching the gate, she ordered her bearers to stop, for she had seen on the wall, still blackened by the fires of the Boxer Rebellion, a crowd of foreigners from the legation quarter who had assembled to watch her historic return. Stepping from her chair, she looked up for a few moments intently at the foreigners; then, with her hands held together under her chin in the Chinese fashion, she made several small bows towards them and the foreigners applauded. Stepping again into her chair she was carried onwards to the Forbidden City.

In the remaining years of her life, the old Empress Dowager showed none of her former hostility towards foreigners. She also instituted a number of long-overdue reforms including the abolition of the practice of extracting confessions by torture in criminal cases. But it was too late. The spirit of the republican movement led by Sun Yat-sen was spreading and it was clear that nothing could prevent the end of the Manchu dynasty.

On November 14th, 1908 the sad and inefficient Kuang-hsu Emperor died – or (as many believe) was poisoned by the Empress Dowager. As a last gesture of spite against those who thought they might inherit the throne, she named Pu Yi, the son of a prince, the successor. He was two years old. For the third time she was placing a child on the imperial throne. Earlier that month she had celebrated her seventy-third birthday; she had every intention, she said, of living longer than Queen Victoria. But on November 15th – the day after the death of the Emperor – Tzu Hsi herself had a seizure and died.

Propped up on pillows, the infant Pu Yi was placed on the Dragon Throne in the Forbidden City and surrounded by the pomp and ceremony due to the rulers of the Celestial Empire. He was destined to remain there only three years, for now province after province was declaring its independence of the Manchu court and giving its support to Sun Yat-sen. The pretence of imperial authority could no longer be sustained and on February 7th, 1912, the child Emperor abdicated. The line of Chinese emperors that had stretched back for 2,700 years had finally petered out.

Pu Yi, without power or influence, but still surrounded by concubines and eunuchs, was allowed to live on in the Forbidden City until 1924, when he was seventeen years old.

The long, turbulent story of Peking was not yet over, for in 1937 the city was once more overrun and occupied – this time by the army of Japan, after that country had launched its massive invasion of China. Chiang Kai-shek's Kuomintang troops evacuated the City art treasures and the universities and then abandoned Peking to the Japanese who occupied the city until their defeat at the end of the Second World War. The ex-Emperor Pu Yi, living in the north-east had meanwhile become a puppet of the Japanese. He did not return to Peking until 1950.

During the Civil War which followed the defeat of the Japanese, at a time when the Communist armies were forcing the Kuomintang to retreat to the south (and eventually to Taiwan), Mao Tsetung was determined that Peking would be liberated in a manner that would not damage the city. Thus his armies made no attempt to storm the city but instead they flowed around it, leaving it an isolated outpost until the Kuomintang defenders capitulated.

Time can play some strange tricks. So much happened since the fall

Sun Yat-sen – the founder of the Chinese Republic after the fall of the Chinese Empire.

Pu Yi – the last Emperor of China.

of the Manchu dynasty that one tends to think of the Imperial Chinese Empire, with all its weird traditions and feudal tyranny as belonging to some far-distant age. Yet, in fact, it was only fifteen years or so ago that I myself met the last Emperor of China – in, of all places, a crowded Peking bus during the rush hour. I had met him briefly once before some years earlier. I remembered him as an elderly, slightly stooped man who, while shaking hands, peered at me through thick spectacles. Now surely this man sitting immediately in front of me on the bus was the same gentleman. To make sure, I nudged Yao Wei, my interpreter, and pointed discreetly at the elderly passenger dressed in blue work clothes. 'Isn't that Pu Yi?' I whispered. Yao Wei nodded.

By an amazing coincidence we happened at that moment to be passing the long northern wall of the Forbidden City. I couldn't resist it. I leaned forward. 'Excuse me, Mr Pu Yi, but how does it feel to be sitting here in a crowded bus while passing the Palace where you were brought up with a thousand servants at your beck and call?'

He must have heard this kind of question many times before, for he had the appropriate answer ready. 'Ah', he said, 'I am much freer now than I was then. In *there* [pointing at the Palace] I was like a prisoner. Now I'm free to take an ordinary bus like this and move about among the masses.'

This then, in brief outline, is the imperial history of Peking. We have seen how, through all the turbulence, the city survived. The people of Peking indeed did more than survive; they kept their 'Chineseness'. Peking, and most of China, was ruled by non-Han Chinese* for 800 of the past 1,000 years. The Hans were overcome by superior military forces, but they were then faced with more formidable opposition – the capacity of the Han Chinese for urbane and implacable resistance. Emperors soon found that they had to appoint Han Chinese advisers if they were to get things done. To appear less foreign they adopted Han dress and manners. They retained the traditional way of administering the country. They even prayed for fine harvests in Han temples.

For their part, the Hans continued their own traditions in architecture, art and music and their belief in Confucian principles of behaviour. In this way, despite many invasions, the most recent of which was that of the Japanese in the last war, and despite innumerable disasters, the continuum of Han Chinese civilization in all essentials

---

* The majority of people in China are of Han nationality. But China now consists of over fifty minority nationalities. Those who 'invaded' Han territory – the people of Mongolia and Manchuria – are today equal members of the 'family of nationalities' that make up China.

was maintained. As Andrew Boyd, the architectural historian, has pointed out, there has been in China,

> straight from the bronze age right up to the present, a completely continuous, individual and self-conscious civilization of an extremely high level: one might say one nation with (basically) one language, one script, one literature, one system of ethical concepts, one tradition in the arts ...

It is this sheer *continuity* that I feel around me when I am in Peking, and it stuns my Western mind. I find it impossible to imagine what it must be like to be part of a civilization that stretches back uninterruptedly for thirty-five centuries. Even the forms of government established 2,500 years ago remained virtually unaltered until well into the present century. It is as if the House of Commons had been functioning as it does today since before the Roman conquest, or the American Constitution had been written before the time of Christ. This range of historical perspective is beyond me, I find it inconceivable. But it must be present somewhere in the deeper consciousness of the Chinese. With this history of survival-against-all-odds, no wonder the people of Peking appear so certain of themselves and so unshakeably confident in the new society they are building. They must feel they are citizens of an immortal city!

Throughout those many years the people never for a moment forgot that the emperors who issued orders from inside those palace walls were not Han Chinese. They submitted not because they wished to but because they must, and they would bide their time with patient but relentless determination for the moment when they could be rid of them. This is the origin, perhaps, of one of the most marked characteristics of the Chinese – their profound resistance to all foreign influence, a determination to hold to their own ways, their own ideas and their own principles, regardless of all pressures and all expediencies. This trait continues to the present day in large matters and in small. It is seen in their relationships with other countries and in their often bland disregard of any outside suggestion that in this matter or that they might usefully modify their ways. Except on strictly technical subjects I have seldom been asked how this or that is done in other countries. The people of Peking today are very certain where they are going and they will go there in their own way. This trait often baffles or infuriates foreigners, who regard it as rigidity or mere stubbornness, but at bottom it is the source of China's massive powers of endurance and her strength.

4 Four Centuries in
One Generation

'People abroad', a senior government official, a woman, told me, 'still think of Peking as a kind of antique shop. Look around and you will see how mistaken they are.'

She was right.

The great Imperial City, isolated within its wall, remains the dominating feature of Peking; and the hundreds of little lanes, the *hutungs*, with their intimate and friendly courtyards, remind us of what so much of the city was like not so many years ago.

Peking, until relatively recent times, was contained within a series of walls, and was, in fact, four cities in one (see the map on p. 54). The upper rectangle is the Inner City (sometimes called 'The Tartar City') in which, like boxes within a box, lie the Imperial City and within that, the Forbidden City. This was the part of Peking built by Yung-lo in the Ming dynasty, which we described in the last chapter. The lower rectangle is the 'Outer City' (sometimes referred to as 'The Chinese City') which was built about a century later, in 1553, to accommodate and protect a growing population. There were six gates to the Inner City and seven to the Outer, each with a high and imposing guard house above it. Three gates penetrated the wall that divided the Outer from the Inner City, the most imposing one of which was Chienmen lying on the central north–south axis along which lay all the most important gates and palaces. For nearly four centuries these walls defined the area of Peking. Even as recently as the 1930s, the gates of the city were closed at night to protect the citizens against bandits and evil spirits.

On each of my visits during the past twenty-two years I have seen the city burgeoning ever further outward beyond its walls. There are lovers of antiquities who have been saddened and even outraged to see so many of these walls and great gates being demolished to make room for the city's expansion, for new roads, new buildings. But as we have seen, the people of Peking have a long history of pulling things down to start again. Today, the municipal area of Greater Peking is 16,800 square kilometres, making it larger in area than any city in the world. It is possible to drive in a straight line for 150 kilometres and still be in Peking.

Some 'old China hands' who knew Peking before the revolution have told me that when they returned they could hardly recognize the city, so greatly had its character changed. They missed the sights and smells of the crowded city streets as they knew them then – the cries of the street vendors carrying their wares on shoulder poles, the thousands of stalls and tiny shops that lined the main streets, the creaking horse carts, the smoke rising from open ovens where passers-by could purchase roasted chestnuts or sweet potatoes cooked in their yellow skins. They missed the game of haggling, trying to buy at the cheapest possible price, and the search for old and valuable curios, priceless scrolls and porcelains which could often be bought for a song.

One or two of the old-timers frankly admit that they still miss the easy life and the comforts foreigners could formerly enjoy – the numerous obedient servants, the exclusive clubs to which Chinese were not admitted, the cosy dinner parties, the rivalry between hostesses to see whose chef could produce the most exotic and delectable dishes. What very few remember, or if they do, choose not to mention, is the abject poverty, the numerous child prostitutes, the stink of the many streets that had no sewerage, the rickshaw 'boys' whose working life expectancy was just eight years, the mothers standing outside the luxury restaurants with outstretched hands and babies in their arms whining with hunger. And the diseased, the many beggars, and in winter the sight of the homeless, huddled in doorways wrapped in newspapers, and the carts that would come in the morning to collect those who had perished in the cold.

When the new government took over in 1949, the greater part of Peking was in a state of the utmost degradation and squalor. Runaway inflation had made the currency virtually meaningless. A pair of shoes that cost 7 million ¥ (*yuan*) one morning, might cost twenty million the next.* In the whole of Peking only five old buses were operational. Two-thirds of the population had no running water and many had to fetch it in wooden buckets from far away. The well-to-do Chinese and the foreigners, of course, lived on paved streets with sanitation and a water supply to each house. In 1949 there were, in fact, 200 kilometres of sewerage pipes – some dating from the Ming dynasty – but, due to neglect, only twenty kilometres were usable.

* This is no exaggeration. Between 1937 and 1949, commodity prices increased 8½ million times. Money that would buy twelve oxen in 1937 would not buy a single grain of rice in 1949.

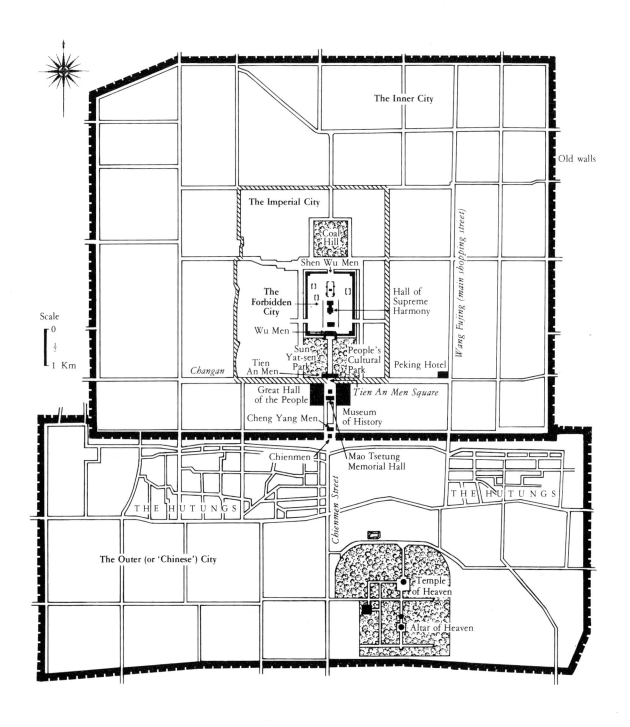

The Inner City

Old walls

The Imperial City

Coal Hill

Shen Wu Men

The Forbidden City

Hall of Supreme Harmony

Wu Men

Wang Fujing (main shopping street)

Scale
0
½
1 Km

Changan

Tien An Men

Sun Yat-sen Park

People's Cultural Park

Peking Hotel

Great Hall of the People

Tien An Men Square

Cheng Yang Men

Museum of History

Chienmen

Mao Tsetung Memorial Hall

Chienmen Street

T H E   H U T U N G S

T H E   H U T U N G S

The Outer (or 'Chinese') City

Temple of Heaven

Altar of Heaven

Central Peking today, showing the old walls
(now almost gone) and the Imperial and Forbidden Cities.

In the Outer (or 'Chinese') City especially, conditions were appalling. There was almost no electricity, no laid-on water. The only means of sewage disposal were open ditches which, after heavy rainfall, would overflow and seep into the houses. The *hutungs* were unpaved and as there was no regular system of collection, garbage and refuse would sometimes pile up a metre deep. For the vast majority of people in Peking there were no modern medical facilities at all. The housing conditions for many were unspeakably wretched – some families even lived in cave-like holes dug into the city walls. There were 250 brothels in the city.

That was the legacy. That, in 1949, was the state of the capital of the nation with the largest population in the world.

Conditions would have been very much like this in Paris or London in the sixteenth century. Perhaps the most astonishing fact about Peking is that the advances made in the European cities during the last 400 years are being accomplished in Peking in a single generation.

For the new national government, one of the first priorities was to stabilize the currency. For the Peking administration, the immediate job was to clean up the city. Tens of thousands of people, mostly drawn from among the unemployed, were mobilized, with shovels, handcarts and as many horse carts as could be mustered. Before long, thousands of tonnes of accumulated garbage were cleared from the city streets.

Despair and lethargy gave way to action. Buses and trams were repaired so that 164 were in running order even before the end of 1949. (Trams were later abolished; today there are 2,391 buses and electric trolley-buses in operation, all of them made in Peking.) Since 1949 over 2,000 kilometres of water pipe have been laid, bringing drinkable water to all the population. Nearly 1,300 kilometres of new sewer pipes now provide sanitation facilities for the entire city. Several immense electric generating plants provide power for everyone; and central hot-water stations bring hot water and heating to many public buildings; the rest have their own boiler rooms.

The initial 'clean-up' campaign was only the first of many in which the citizens of Peking were rallied to make their city healthy. There was, for example, the great anti-fly campaign in which the entire population of Peking, with fly-swats in hand, declared war on the common fly, and at the same time cleaned out any corner which might become a breeding ground. So thorough was this campaign that even today a fly is hardly ever seen; and any bold enough to appear is attacked immediately.

The civic energy generated by campaigns such as these soon widened into many other areas. There were campaigns against the use of drugs,

Above, the centre of old Peking; *below*, for the majority, living conditions in pre-revolutionary Peking were appalling.

Right, it was because of poverty such as this that Mao Tsetung at his revolutionary headquarters in Yenan was preparing to overthrow the old order.

against venereal disease and against prostitution. Each of these was treated strictly as a medical and social and not as a moral problem. If those afflicted were to be persuaded to come forward for treatment, the first essential was to eliminate their sense of guilt. With newspaper articles, radio broadcasts, wall posters, magazines and neighbourhood meetings, an immense educational campaign was launched to convince the public that those afflicted were victims of the old society. They must not be blamed, nor must they blame themselves, for circumstances that were forced upon them.

Hospitals were set up for the drug addicts; special homes were established for former prostitutes where they were helped to re-establish their self-respect and where they could learn some useful skill. These girls were urged never to hide their former trade, even from those they might later wish to marry.

To tackle venereal disease, which was very widespread, Wasserman tests were given to anyone who suspected that he might have contracted the disease and treatment was prescribed for tens of thousands. Wassermans continued to be given as a routine measure to everyone who attended any clinic or hospital. The practice was discontinued only after several years of 100 *per cent* negative findings – venereal disease in Peking has been eliminated (as it has been throughout China).

There were many other campaigns. The anti-spitting campaign, for example. Spitting in China was almost a national habit and I remember the campaign launched to end it.* Again, massive publicity was co-ordinated to educate the public to the ill effects of spitting–the spreading of tuberculosis, for instance. Teenagers were mobilized and all over Peking one could see them holding up small placards on bamboo sticks and handing out leaflets to passers-by. In ways such as these, using every possible means of education, some very deep-seated social habits have been altered. *These campaigns had a purpose that went beyond the immediate need for improved standards of cleanliness and health–they were a demonstration of what could be accomplished by collective social effort and they thus had a political relevance as well.*

Industry in Peking in 1949 was negligible. There was a workshop producing a small amount of pig-iron (but no steel); there was a small coal mine, a railway-carriage repair shop, a woollen textile mill, a power plant and a brewery set up by the Japanese during their occupation of the city. In addition, there were handicrafts shops, blacksmiths, furniture repair shops, but these were all on the smallest scale. China in

---

*In recent visits I have noticed the habit of spitting is beginning to reassert itself – perhaps a new anti-spitting campaign should be launched?

those days was known as the 'sick man of Asia', more backward, more poverty-stricken than India. Peking, the capital, reflected this general industrial backwardness—much more so than Shanghai, a city whose business was dominated by foreigners. Peking, with almost no industrial facilities, had to buy whatever was required either from abroad or from other cities in China (even matches, which used to be called *Yang huo*—meaning 'foreign fire'). It was essentially a *consumer* city.

Starting, then, from scratch the people of Peking set out to become a major centre of production. They have now constructed over 2,000 factories, some very large, and almost all of them working two, and some three, shifts a day. The small pig-iron workshop has been transformed into a great steel complex producing not only ordinary steel but 10,000 varieties of high-grade alloy steels. A city that had no machine shop—not even of the simplest kind required for building bicycles—now has 400 machine-tool factories of all sizes manufacturing over 200,000 parts. Peking today manufactures virtually all the domestic requirements of her citizens, including sewing machines, bicycles, refrigerators, television sets (both black and white and colour), cameras, watches and pharmaceutical goods. Computers and a great variety of precision instruments are now being manufactured. Within Greater Peking is a truck and jeep factory (jeeps are called *jee-pu*), a plant for making large-scale electric generators, an oil refinery employing 24,000 people, three huge textile plants and forty smaller ones producing cotton, woollen, silk and a great variety of synthetic goods. Peking formerly had no chemical plant except for a small workshop making fireworks for children; today the city manufactures the complete range of chemicals required for modern industry.

One day some Chinese officials from the Peking municipal administration, took Elena and me to the roof of one of the new multi-storey apartment houses, and from there we could see how large the city had become. Looking east, with the ancient palaces behind us, we looked across rows upon rows of workers' apartment blocks, and beyond them new industries, new factories as far as our eyes could see.

'Industries', 'factories'. For most Westerners these words conjure up a picture of smoke and dirt, the appalling monotony of assembly-lines, the reflected glare in the sky at night of giant blast furnaces, the infernal din of cotton mills, and millions of workers held in the new slavery of our mechanized societies. Looking across that industrial landscape of Peking, I wondered whether this city wouldn't in the end become just another Pittsburgh or Manchester. For factories are factories wherever they are, except that the newer ones in Peking produce less smoke, for

Previous page, Shen Wu Men, the northern gate, through which the Empress Dowager escaped during the Boxer Rebellion.

Facing page, all that remains of the old Summer Palace, and *below*, the Pearl Necklace Bridge in the grounds of the palace.

Right, restoring the statuary along the Great Spirit Way, and *below*, a tomb of the Ming emperors.

Following page, the bronze lion in the Forbidden City.

the Chinese have been learning from our mistakes and recently have begun to build their factories with built-in anti-pollution devices. (The older factories still belch black smoke!)

I realized that our companions were seeing these factories with quite different eyes and with none of my doubts. The Chinese have no nostalgia for the past, for it treated them badly, and they are quite ready to replace the 'charm' of old Peking for something more relevant to their needs. 'Industry' is an exciting word to those who have suffered too long from the lack of it.

The saving grace, making bearable what would otherwise have been a scene of unrelieved dreariness, was the trees. Interspersed among the blocks of flats, shielding the stark outline of the factories and in rows along every street, was the green foliage of countless trees.

I knew from photographs taken before 1949 that Peking was then almost a treeless city. By the time I first went there more than twenty years ago, I was already impressed by the number of small saplings that had been planted everywhere. As I reported at the time:

> Trees everywhere . . . trees line every street and not just a sober row or two along each avenue but eight rows or ten or twelve. Down one new avenue behind the walls I counted trees *twenty* rows deep on either side. Around Tian An Men they have not planted small trees and waited for them to grow but brought in grown ones, pines and evergreens, roots carefully boxed. Not just a few but hundreds. One day I watched several more coming in on a truck and a giant crane lifting them each in turn and lowering them gently, into the waiting cavity below.

I was so impressed by this that I asked the municipal authorities how many trees had been planted in all. They could not give us an immediate answer, for the information had to be obtained from several departments. Later they brought us the figures. Up to the end of 1976, in the central districts of Peking and in the immediate suburbs, 24 million trees had been planted; in all of Greater Peking just over 200 million trees had been planted. Staggering as these figures are, I could believe them.

'How was it done?' I asked.

They described how a tree-planting campaign had been organized soon after liberation. Thousands of people took part. Schools, for example, arranged for their students to plant and be responsible for a certain number of trees and for tending them until they were established. Factory workers planted trees around their workshops, residents organized tree-planting parties for their block of apartments. The municipal authorities brought in saplings from the country and gave advice – the people did the rest. Even today, every year more trees are planted.*

To change a city such as Peking in so short a time from a non-industrial community to a manufacturing city – the fifth largest production centre in China – needed more than collective enthusiasm and a readiness to work. Behind the astonishing progress lies an immense amount of intricate and skilful planning. Peking's development has to be integrated with the nation's over-all requirement as projected in successive five-year plans. Planning was absolutely essential; but an equally important ingredient for success was the social and political principles on which this planning was based. 'Politics in Command' thus became the watchword.

The word 'politics' as used by the Chinese bears no correspondence at all to the *party* rivalries which we associate with politics. Politics to the Chinese is the ideology which will determine the decisions and behaviour, the very consciousness, of people both in small matters and in large. The changes that have taken place in China didn't come out of thin air; they came through the slow education of the people. Mao Tsetung's genius lay in his capacity to take his people step by step from where they were and in his ability to put his teachings into simple words which all could understand. And they accepted them and applied them *because they worked*. He adapted Marxism to the Chinese social structure, drawing from the past and learning from the errors of the West.

Anyone strolling through the streets of Peking or walking through a factory will have noticed everywhere brilliantly painted posters and slogans. These provide, in a kind of shorthand, China's basic political direction. Some of the slogans, SERVE THE PEOPLE; FIGHT SELF INTEREST, we would probably consider ethical exhortations, but to the Chinese they are *political* slogans, for they believe that personal attitudes and behaviour are an integral part of politics.

For me, the most telling slogan of all is TRUST THE PEOPLE, for to trust the people is to allow them to participate and be a part of the decision-making process.† Not by electing representatives to make the decisions for them, but in numberless concrete issues that arise during work in the factories and the agricultural communities.

*In 1977 alone another 600,000 trees were planted, 470,000 by voluntary labour. In the spring of 1978 another 480,000.

†Except, it seems, at the very highest national level. The inner-government struggle after the

60

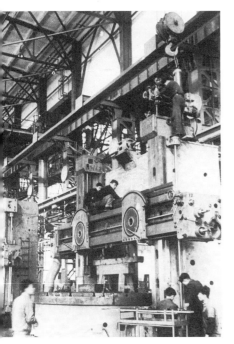

Inside a steel mill, and working on a harp in the musical instrument factory in Peking.

A factory, of course, remains a factory, and routine work remains arduous whether in Peking or Pittsburgh. But the crucial difference between the factories we saw in China and those in the West are the *social relations* in them, the elimination of social distinction between those who give orders and those who carry them out. Without the active and enthusiastic participation of the workers, the industrial advances could not, I feel certain, have been achieved.

The Chinese are the first to admit that the development of a new social consciousness does not come overnight. They realize that the revolution, the struggle, is not yet over. They are still struggling, for example, to remove what they call the 'three differences' – the difference between conditions in the city and conditions in the country; the difference in attitude towards mental work and manual work. These, to the Chinese, are not abstract concepts; the struggle for them is real enough and arises every day in all kinds of practical situations.

deaths of Mao Tsetung and Chou En-lai indicated how little the general public was involved. China has not yet developed constitutional procedures for the passing on of power on the basis of popular representation as we know it. Perhaps she will in time find a better way than our so-called democratic procedures, which are often democratic in form but not in substance.

FIGHT SELF INTEREST ('What's in it for me?') does not refer only to
the idea 'What's in it for me personally?' but to 'What's in it for our
factory?' or 'What's in it for our Commune?' Do we agree to an
industrial plan that might help another factory more than ours? Are we
ready to share our irrigation water with a neighbouring Commune? We
in the West have experienced this kind of co-operation, for during
periods of great national crisis, such as war, we see this same kind of
readiness of individuals to forget their own personal interests and
commit themselves wholly to major national goals.

To give another example: there is still a constant struggle between
what the Chinese call the 'two lines'. In a factory there are those who
want genuine workers' control and those who believe that for the sake
of 'efficiency' management should be exercised by experts. There are
those who still consider mental work inherently superior to manual
work and feel it should be more highly rewarded, and there are others
who think that an individual's mental capacity is not a form of 'private
property' that should be specially paid for. Every one in China today
recognizes that the country needs highly qualified men and women in
all fields. What they don't intend to allow is the notion that such men
and women should consider themselves members of an élite.

Some years ago one was still seeing a slogan clearly intended to build
up the self-confidence of workers: DON'T BE FRIGHTENED OF THE
EXPERTS – COMPETE WITH THEM. I haven't seen this slogan for
some years, for the workers in China today *are* self-confident. They are
not impressed any longer with those who have only book-knowledge;
and even those with book-knowledge are beginning to realize their
limitations. For example, during the Cultural Revolution, professors of
metallurgy working in the steel mills found many instances where
workers who had never even gone to Middle School were solving,
through empirical methods, what they as professors would have considered complicated theoretical problems.

In 1978 the Chinese launched an immense, nation-wide drive to
improve and increase their production and scientific knowledge.
Friends of China hope that the Chinese will not forget what Mao
Tsetung so often emphasized – that 'productivity at any price' or
'efficiency at any price' under élitist management can be self-defeating,
for it omits the essential element of workers' participation. We have
seen in our own societies, and in the Soviet experience, that merely to
'nationalize' an industry while leaving it under the same kind of (or even
worse) bureaucratic management, does nothing to all to release the
enthusiasm and initiative of the workers.

A modern oil refinery in the far outskirts of Greater Peking.

China is the largest producer and the largest exporter of textiles in the world.

The enormous struggle which is known as the Cultural Revolution was precisely between these two lines of thought – between those who said 'The political revolution is over – let's get on with production', and those who said 'The revolution is *not* over, the social distinctions in our society have *not* been fully eliminated and, until they are, politics and not technique must remain in command.' The vast majority of the workers and peasants *know* from everyday, concrete experience that there are still those who want to maintain the old outlook and its procedures. The workers and peasants know that the struggle must continue or they may lose all that they have achieved and again find themselves under bureaucratic control by factory or Commune managers, or by officious government or Party representatives. They will continue to fight to prevent this as they fought, and overthrew, the Gang of Four. This is the reason for the bitter struggles that from time to time erupt in China and which leave the West mystified. They are essentially crucial struggles between two categories of *ideas*, of policies, which will in the end determine what kind of society China will become.

It is an extraordinary experience to see factories run by workers' committees. On this recent journey we visited a textile plant, a motor vehicle factory, a brewery, a carpet factory, a newspaper, an electric generator factory, an oil refinery, a textile mill, a musical instrument factory – a wide spectrum of production activity, and all in Peking. Though each factory varied in size and in the nature of its product, the basic story was the same in all of them.

After the Revolution, very few Chinese had any engineering experience. Almost no mechanical knowledge. At first equipment was imported from the Soviet Union and Europe, and Soviet engineers helped to get the factories started. In 1960 the Soviet engineers were withdrawn due to the sharpening ideological differences between the two countries and the growing Soviet government's attempt to impose Soviet-style 'socialism' upon China.

With the withdrawal of the Soviet engineers – who took their blueprints with them – China was left with several hundred large-scale unfinished projects, several dozen of them in Peking. At the time it appeared a major disaster. Now the Chinese look upon it as a blessing. They learned from this experience that they could not count on other countries but had to work things out for themselves. Once they had paid off, in early 1966, their last indebtedness to the Soviet government the Chinese never again accepted foreign aid, nor allowed foreign investment in China. 'Self-reliance' became a national slogan. A few years ago I had seen many foreign-made machines in the factories. Now, looking carefully at even highly sophisticated machines, I saw that virtually all were of Chinese manufacture. This does not mean that China ever fully rejected Mao's advice to 'learn from abroad', and latterly there is every indication that the Chinese are more ready than they have been since the Soviet engineers departed to hasten their industrial and scientific development with help from the technically more advanced nations. But this will never be done at the price of losing their own basic reliance on themselves.

The directors of the factories we visited were solid, down-to-earth people, accustomed to dealing with realities. They appeared to us, especially considering their responsibilities, to be easy and self-assured with no pretence about them, and very ready to admit how much China still had to learn. In clothes and manner these directors were indistinguishable from the other workers. There was no attempt to put on a show. Except for one large room which the management committee uses for meetings, and in which visitors are given tea and a briefing, the 'front offices' of Peking's factories are shabby. Nothing is wasted on non-essentials. The director's office is usually quite small and is sometimes shared with others.

In the majority of the factories we visited, the directors and the heads of departments had all started as ordinary workers on the shop floor; and it is an accepted principle that *all* managerial staff ('cadres' to the Chinese) including the director would spend at least one full day a week, or its equivalent, taking their place and working along with the others in the factory. I asked the director of a machine-tool factory whether he minded this. He said he didn't. It got him away from desk work and helped him to know what problems there were in the shop. It also enabled him to keep his hand in at the lathes. He was elected to the position of director by the workers, the cadres, and the Party Committee of the factory and they could replace him whenever they wanted. If ever they did, he would easily be able to go back to the work he was doing before.

This director's father was a rickshaw driver before the revolution, and the director himself had no education until after liberation, when he was twenty-two. Then he attended literary classes at the evening schools which were set up throughout Peking. We heard many similar stories in the factories we visited.

This explains the director's easy relations with other workers: he himself was one of them. There were no 'bosses' in the factories we visited, no know-it-all 'experts' to freeze the initiative of the unedu-

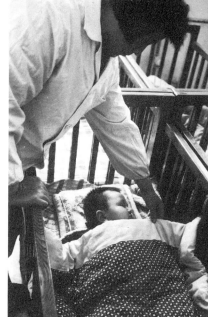

A factory canteen   A factory nursery

cated, for they were *all* in a formal sense 'uneducated'. It also explains why these largely self-taught men and women are dubious about the value of intellectual knowledge that is unrelated to practical experience. During the Cultural Revolution, when the universities were closed, professors of engineering were sent to work in factories for a year or two – another step towards breaking down the mental–manual differences.

I asked about wage differentials. 'We have not reached the stage where we can do away with differences in pay,' we were told, 'though that will eventually come when we are more politically advanced.' The industrial workers have an eight-tier wage scale. The difference between the highest and lowest paid worker in a factory is normally three to one; in some cases it is as high as five or six to one. Pay varies according to the skills a man or woman has mastered, not status. Thus a director might earn less than others in a factory. Although he probably works harder than anyone else, he enjoys no special perquisites or privileges. (This is the *theory*. There are still enough exceptions to make it necessary from time to time to expose the creeping-in of 'bourgeois rights'.) The director lives in the same sized apartment as others, determined by the number in his family. There are no privately owned cars in China, but a director can call on one if he has to travel, say, to an official meeting elsewhere in Peking.

One day Elena and I, with Lü as interpreter, walked home with a worker from a machine-tool factory. His name was Chu. We did not

66

have far to walk. Wherever possible, the workers' living quarters are built within easy walking or bicycling distance of the place where they work. The factory and the apartment houses form a self-contained community with schools, nurseries, shops, a cinema, medical clinic and so on

Chu lived in one of those rows of indistinguishable, faceless blocks of apartments that I had seen in the distance from the roof top. There was no grass, only dusty earth between the apartment houses, for Peking is unlucky in its climate. It is too cold in the winter, too hot and dry in the summer for grass to grow. But — there were the trees! In their shade as we went by, we could see children, some playing ping-pong, some basket-ball; old women were sitting in groups, chatting, fanning themselves for the day was very hot. An old man sat nodding in a wicker chair; on the balcony of one apartment a woman was hanging out her washing. Then, up three flights of dark stairs. Chu's wife comes to greet us, wiping her hands on her apron, a shade flustered to see strangers arrive unexpectedly, and two of them foreigners. She welcomes us and then goes off to bring us tea.

I look around. The room is very much the same as dozens of apartments I have been in in Peking — and in the rest of the country. Workers' apartments usually consist of two smallish rooms (three if the family has several children), a kitchen and toilet. Some have bathrooms too, but more often there are large communal shower rooms for each block. The Chus' kitchen is standard — quite small, with no shiny white tiles, or gadgets. Along one wall, a sink with a cold water tap, a shelf with a thick chopping block and a small gas range. Opposite, shelves and cupboards. Nearly all Chinese cooking (except for steamed dishes) is done in two utensils — a large pot for boiling rice and a deeper circular metal bowl with handles (the *guo*) in which almost everything else is cooked after being chopped with a cleaver such as our butchers sometimes use. Nothing is brought to the table that cannot be eaten with chopsticks, so meat and poultry is cut in the kitchen first.

Dull as these apartment buildings are on the outside, the living and bedrooms are invariably colourful, and neat and clean as a pin. The similarity in the appearance of the interiors is striking. Everywhere, it seems, colourful quilts are folded in the same way at the foot of the beds. (All beds in China, except those likely to be used by foreigners, are hard board beds.) Somewhere in every apartment will be a picture or small bust of Mao Tsetung and, since Mao's death, of Hua Kuo-feng. In the room where the family eats there will be a small square table with a vase of artificial flowers; on the sideboard, a brightly decorated

A typical living room in a Peking worker's home.

thermos flask and a tray with tea cups. Every apartment in Peking by now has a radio and more often than not a sewing machine. On one wall there will be pictures from the latest movie and of Tian An Men, and a place where numerous small black and white photographs of family and friends are pinned and kept in view. There are variations. Some families might have a goldfish bowl, some pots of growing plants. But, by and large, the Chinese prefer to do things the same way as others. In home decoration, as in so many other ways, they like to remain, as it were, anonymous, unnoticed, just as one among many. There is no attempt, no rivalry, to be 'different'.

Mr and Mrs Chu both work, Mr Chu at the factory where we met him, Mrs Chu works half-day as a cleaner at a hospital. She leaves for work after seeing their two children off to school in the morning. The Chus' combined incomes would be in the neighbourhood of ¥100 a month – about £33 or $62. This might sound to us a very low income, but as we talked it became clear that they had no difficulty in making ends meet. I could understand why, for the expenses of a worker's family in Peking are also very low. Rent is never more than ¥5 or ¥6 a month (£1.25, $2.37 or £1.50, $2.85), and this would include water and heat. Food presents little financial problem. Both Mr and Mrs Chu eat their midday meal where they work. The standard cost of a meal in a factory canteen is about 15 *fen* or less than 5p (9½¢), and this would include one dish with meat. The children eat at school. Clothes are probably the family's greatest expense, especially with two growing children. I noticed in the passage outside the apartment the two bicycles owned by Mr and Mrs Chu (each of these would have cost them the wages earned in six weeks) and, standing in one corner of the room, was a fairly new foot-treadle sewing-machine. Their basic needs therefore had already been met.

As for medical expenses, both the Chus are fully covered by the places where they work. If the children ever needed medical attention the Chus would have to pay half the cost, but these also, by our standards, are almost unbelievably low. Even if one of the children required hospitalization the cost would be only 30p or 57¢ per day with another 15p or 28¢ for food. The maximum cost of a major operation is £2.45 or $4.65. At retirement – fifty-five for women, sixty for men – workers receive up to eighty per cent of their wage as pension.

So, low though the Chus' wages were, I was not surprised when it came out in conversation that they had almost ¥400 savings in the bank (about £125 or $237). They were planning to use some of the money for a journey to another province to visit Mr Chu's parents.

As we talked, Mrs Chu gave me the impression of being a woman very accustomed to hard work. It is always difficult to judge the age of a Chinese but I would say she was in her late thirties. Her hands, as she held them loosely in her lap, had seen much manual labour. Her parents were peasants and she was brought up in the country.

We stayed about an hour and then took our leave, just as the two girls, in skirts and with bright red scarves around their necks, arrived from school. They shyly shook hands with us in turn. Then we left, Mr and Mrs Chu in Chinese fashion coming down to the front door to see us off.

The Chus (and many other workers too) had mentioned that they had savings in a bank. This, before liberation, would have been inconceivable and I decided to follow it up. So one afternoon we called on the manager of a small neighbourhood bank in what was formerly a poor section of north-west Peking.

There were perhaps fifteen people at the counter. Four girls were attending to them and others were sitting at their desks, each with an abacus. The room was full of the sound of the clickety-clicks as their fingers, with astonishing speed, would operate these wooden calculators. The manager of the bank, Mr Wang, greeted us and took us to his office. We were the first foreigners to have visited the bank. He was bursting with information. After pouring tea and asking after our health, he gave us a brief account of the bank's operations. The bank is open every day, including Sundays and holidays, from nine in the morning to seven at night. As with all stores in Peking, the attendants work in shifts and stagger their days off. Approximately 10,000 households make use of this particular bank and the average savings per household are about ¥700 (or £224, $425). Long-term deposits earn 3·24 per cent interest, short-term deposits somewhat less. With no personal income tax in China, no capital transfer tax (estate duties) and no buying on credit, there is a natural incentive for families to place any surplus money in a bank. As part of the policy of 'serving the people' the bank had held eight public meetings in the neighbourhood during the previous year so that residents could express their ideas on how the bank's service could be improved.

We then discussed inflation. From the records I had kept since my first visit to Peking twenty-two years ago, I knew that the prices in the shops for basic commodities now were precisely the same as they were then, except for certain items which now cost *less*. (There are a few exceptions. Surprisingly, fruit is somewhat dearer than formerly.) I asked Mr Wang how China was able to avoid inflation. He said he had read about the problem of rising prices in Western countries. His explanation of how China had avoided this was simple. To avoid inflation the state plans its production so that the value of the consumer goods for sale always exceeds the total money supply paid out in wages. What makes this possible, Mr Wang explained, is that the country has no foreign debt (beyond a small debt covering current commercial activities), nor is there any foreign investment in China. Thus the government can plan the nation's economy quite independently of outside influence or pressure.*

I asked the bank manager to explain the country's tax structure, how the government derives its income for current expenditures on education, the army, the medical services, roads and so on; and for its capital expenditure on factories, hospitals, and other major construction. He

---

*The lack of foreign debt has great significance. Almost all 'third world' countries are very heavily in debt to foreign governments or foreign business concerns. This indebtedness becomes a millstone, inhibiting local economic development, for enormous sums have to be set aside for repayment or servicing of this debt. China paid back her last foreign debt – to the Soviet Union – early in 1966. Since then she has been free to plough back any national surplus into a further development of her own economy.

A family in industrial Peking – all work in the same factory: 1 mother in the hospital; 2 father in the printing works; 3 younger son at the factory middle school; 4 elder son studies for examinations; 5 elder daughter tends a machine; 6 younger daughter in control centre.

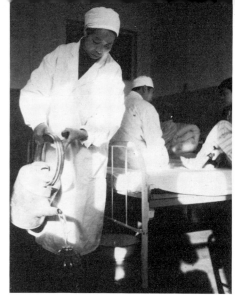

2

3

5

4

told me that there are eight kinds of taxes, some of which I had never heard of before. There is a tax, for instance, on salt production, another on slaughterhouses. There are licence fees for vehicles and shops and, of course, customs duties. There is a tax on agriculture – usually about seven per cent of a Commune's production is taken for tax. By far the largest proportion of the state's income comes from profits earned by state-owned enterprises. Indeed, ninety-nine per cent of the funds required by the government come from state enterprises and those sections of the economy under collective ownership. The individual himself does not have to fill out personal income tax forms; but he pays more for the things he buys than they actually cost to make – and this 'profit' is used for running and developing the country.

Under this system, he explained, the government can vary the tax according to the needs of the population. Products to improve the health of the people, medicines for example, are sold at exactly what it costs to make them and the state makes no profit on them at all; and as the cost of producing them goes down, so the cost to the public is likewise reduced. Some medicines are now sold for much less than they were only a few years ago. (Penicillin, for example, is only fifty-eight per cent of what it was ten years ago. Taken as a whole medicines now, on average, cost only eighteen per cent of what they were in 1952.) Everyday necessities are cheap, and the tax on them is kept low, although a small profit margin is maintained. Coal, for example, has gone down in the last twenty years from ¥2.80 (90p, $1.70) per 50 kilograms to ¥2.50 (80p, $1.50). In the case of non-essentials (cameras, cosmetics, small transistor radios, colour television sets), the prices are relatively high and those are maintained even if production costs come down – the higher profit on these helping to keep the essential commodities cheap. Investment in light industry brings a rapid return which then provides funds for investment in heavy industry. The relations between heavy and light industrial development are thus not the same in China as they were in the Soviet Union, which emphasized heavy at the cost of light industrial development.

After this brief but enlightening lecture in basic economics, we said goodbye. On the way out I noticed a colourful poster on the wall: TAKE AN ACTIVE PART IN PUTTING MONEY IN THE BANK TO HELP SOCIALIST CONSTRUCTION.

The rapidity with which the Chinese have mastered modern technology shouldn't really surprise us, for they have had a long history of inventiveness and mechanical skill. It was, after all, the Chinese who first discovered the useful properties of a black rock which we call coal.

'Take an active part in putting money in the bank to help socialist construction.'

While Europeans were eating off wooden platters, they were making bowls in a material as delicate as egg shells which we still call 'china'. Even the homely wheelbarrow was used in China 1,000 years before someone in Europe stumbled on the same idea. The Chinese made an instrument which was the father of all seismographs 400 years before the Persians. One thousand years before the Arabs they had an intricate knowledge of the movement of the stars and planets. And what did the Italians eat before Marco Polo brought noodles back from China?

I find the list of Chinese inventions and discoveries fascinating. Here are a few others, and I have indicated how many centuries it was before the Europeans caught up!

	Centuries before the West
The cross-bow as a weapon	13
Porcelain	11–13
Iron suspension bridge	10–13
The kite	12
Cast-iron	10–12
Deep drilling	11
The magnetic compass	11
Paper	10
Canal lock gates	7–17
Gunpowder	5–6
Movable type	4
Stern-post rudder	4

The Chinese also understood the correlation between sun-spots and severe winters; they knew the earth was round a century before Copernicus; and they kept records of eclipses from 1400 B.C.

With this kind of inventiveness, it is equally interesting, and surprising, to note that the screw, invented in the West, didn't reach China for fourteen centuries; the principle of the crankshaft for three centuries; and clockwork, also for three centuries.

In the park near our hotel is one of those strange hills of earth I had noticed while walking around Peking. On my previous visit I had seen truck-load after truck-load of soil being dumped there – it came from the underground shelters which were then being built. Now this hill of earth was being landscaped with rocks and shrubs and many lovely trees, and a winding path that leads to its summit.

I had heard talk about the underground city which had been built below Peking and, indeed, beneath every city in China. In 1969, during the Vietnam War at a time of growing international tensions, when China felt that she herself might be in danger of attack, it was decided that the population of all the major cities should be given protection against blast and atomic fall-out, and this was to be done without interruption of the massive construction that was going on *above* ground. Peking, as did all the other Chinese cities, drew up plans for air-raid shelters on a scale unequalled, as far as I know, anywhere.

Below Peking there is now a vast interconnected network of tunnels and chambers, all lined with concrete and brick. Every shop, factory, office building, theatre, cinema, hotel, school, hospital, has its own entrance, and each tunnel is connected with the others. In various directions passages have been built that run far into the country so that the entire population of the city, if need arises, can be evacuated without exposure.

We asked to see these shelters and the necessary arrangements were made, but with the strict understanding that no photographs were to be taken. To our surprise we were taken to a crowded clothing store in one of Peking's busiest streets. I was wondering why we were there when, to our astonishment, the floor in front of our feet silently slid away, revealing a flight of steps leading down into the ground. Immediately there came into my mind the picture of Ali Baba standing in front of a huge rock and calling 'Open Sesame!' and with these words the rock opening to reveal a wondrous cave. Descending the steps from the clothing store I felt was an experience every bit as enthralling as entering Ali Baba's cave. We walked along the wide, well-lit passages and were astounded at the sheer magnitude of the undertaking. The

A girl worker in the interior of a huge electric generator.

In the Peking jeep factory.

The most popular slogan: 'Serve the people.'

Facing page, top, everyone helps in the fields at harvest time. *Bottom*, a school playground in rural Peking.

A Peking carpet factory.

Rural scenes: *above*, a family at the village pond, and *below*, feeding the ducks.

tunnels themselves are only part of the subterranean structures. We were shown assembly halls, dining rooms, kitchens, facilities for food storage, telephone and broadcasting headquarters, toilets, emergency power generators, first-aid clinics, operating rooms. Deep water wells had been dug, air filtering systems installed; and blast doors set at intervals could isolate sections of the shelter system. The underground network that we examined that afternoon was built for the protection of the people who might in an emergency be caught while shopping or walking in the street immediately above us. There are forty-five shops in this street, and surveys showed that at the most crowded period of the day there might be 10,000 people that would need protection. Plans therefore called for shelter accommodation for that number, and everyone, it was specified, must be able to be below ground within six minutes. 'We had air-raid drills,' our guide told us, 'and we found that the street and shops could be emptied in five and a half minutes.'

This whole system was built by volunteer labour, by workers coming after hours on their day off, and it was completed in four years. There was no difficulty in recruiting volunteers, for the people knew that the shelters were for their own protection. Eighteen hundred people took part in building this one section.

As we made our way back to our original entrance – we had been below ground for about an hour – I wondered where else but in China such an immense collective undertaking could be mounted. At the entrance, the door – again as if by magic – opened and we emerged once more into the shop where people were unconcernedly buying shirts and trousers. Silently behind us the door slid shut and no one looking at it could have guessed what lay below.

That evening in our room at the hotel, Elena and I tried to put into some kind of order the mass of factual material we had been gathering about the new Peking. What was the human meaning that lay behind all the statistics in our notebooks? In the weeks since we stood on the rooftop and looked across the new industrial landscape, we had been to many factories and we were arranging to go to more. We had talked with managers and workers and technicians, and visited some of them in their homes. One thing was absolutely clear – the poverty and degradation of the past was now just an ugly memory. Though still poor, the people of this city, through their own enormous efforts, have transformed their lives.

Further speculation, we reminded ourselves, had better be post- poned, for we had yet to see the other forty-eight per cent of the population – the peasants who live in 'rural Peking'.

5 Rural Peking

The hot, hot summer has come and the winds are blowing in from across the Gobi Desert. This is the Peking summer that foreigners dread and which the Chinese, judging by their unflagging vitality, hardly seem to notice. There are moments now when the sky darkens suddenly and rainstorms sweep across the city, but they bring only very brief relief. In the hotel dining rooms at the Hsin Chiao Hotel the fans are now whirring incessantly, and yesterday – a sure sign that summer is here – the girl attendants appeared in skirts instead of trousers. In the streets the old ladies who tend the lollie stands have to send repeatedly for new supplies. Blue is now 'out'. For men, short-sleeved shirts; for women, light blouses are the summer fashion. Yes, it's hot, and in this hotel there is no air conditioning. At midnight, one sleepless night, I notice that the thermometer stands at 34°C (93°F).

After a long day's shooting in a factory, Yu Ma and Lü came up to our room for a cool drink. As usual we discussed the day's shooting, the mishaps and lucky shots, and future plans. I said, 'Let's forget the city for a while and go and see the Communes in the country.' 'Good,' they agreed, and promised to make the necessary arrangements.

Some readers may at this point be saying to themselves, 'This book is about Peking – not about the countryside.' But, as I've mentioned, Peking includes large areas of the countryside, half the population – forty-seven and a half per cent to be exact – live in the country, which must surely make it the largest 'rural' city in the world!

The 272 Communes that form a part of the municipal area of Peking are not really typical of Communes elsewhere (there are 50,000 in all of China). They are too close to a great metropolis, too near the capital itself, not to be influenced by the active social and industrial life of the city. In these Communes, city and country tend to intermingle. Factories rise up from wheat fields, multiple power lines stretch from pylon to pylon over the paddies. With many small factories and workshops set near the villages, one senses here more than elsewhere the first breaking down of the enormous differences that once existed between the mode of life of the city and the country people.

Yet the basic work of these Communes, like Communes everywhere, is the production of food. The city may be near, but this is unmistakably peasant country. Drive out from Peking in any direction and soon city streets will give way to fields of wheat and rice and vegetables – wide expanses of gold and green as neat and as carefully tended as a garden. Countless numbers of men and women, straw-hatted, are in the fields, working in groups. Some are hoeing between the rows of vegetables; others, with trousers rolled up above the knee and almost knee-deep in water, are stooping, pressing each small rice seedling into the mud, row upon row being spaced with almost mechanical precision. At a nearby pond a man is throwing food to a thousand quacking ducks, still others are clearing irrigation ditches. The work is arduous, as peasant work is everywhere. No one works hurriedly; it is just steady, persistent, rhythmic toil continued hour after hour, year after year. Among peasants there is no separation of 'my own time' and 'work time'. Work is a part of life itself.

Between the fields, small canals fed by electric pumps set above deep wells bring fertility and life to land that would otherwise in summer remain parched. Simple wooden sluices are adjusted to allow the exact amount of water required to flow into the rice paddies; and from that paddy it will flow to the next and then the next – a marvel of intricate irrigation control.* In the vegetable fields, silver rivulets trickle between each row of runner beans and cabbages.

We turn off the main road along a lane running between two fields. Horse carts and trucks are being piled high with vegetables brought in baskets by peasant men and girls from the fields – cabbages, egg-plant, cucumbers, tomatoes, onions, leeks – to be taken to the central markets in the city. We pass men pushing loaded wheelbarrows; girls on their way to the rice paddies balancing huge bunches of rice seedlings on shoulder poles that bend with the weight at every step. Everywhere the ceaseless movement of numberless people at work, the unending activity of China's peasants, the huge, slow-moving, irresistible peasant vitality.

It is now mid-morning, and here and there in the fields groups of workers are breaking off for a rest. They come together and sit on their haunches in a casual circle. Leaving the car we stroll across to one such

---

* The Chinese, of course, led the world in canal construction – the longest canal of the ancient world was the 1,700-kilometre Grand Canal from Peking to Hangchou, begun in 540 B.C. and not completed until the thirteenth century.

One of the many literacy classes set up for adults in the early 1950s.

group. They nod a welcome and with a gesture, invite us to sit. They wipe the lip of an enamel cup, fill it with water from a jug and pass it to us, and cigarettes are offered too. (Again the difference – here, near Peking they have seen foreigners before and take our presence without surprise; deeper in the country it would probably have caused restraint and silence.) We exchange a few questions and then they talk again among themselves, with an occasional burst of laughter. I look at their deeply tanned faces, their muscle-bound hands, their patched clothes, the sweat bands across their foreheads and I feel an immediate liking and respect for them. These men and women have a knowledge of earth and things that grow, knowledge handed down from countless generations, a wisdom far deeper than any book can give. They live with, are almost a part of, the rain and sun and the changing seasons; they know the soil and what it will provide for human life if it is respected and not abused. There is nothing soft about these people; they are not taken in by words. They look at things straight. They know they are poor, but they judge what they have by what they had before.

I have often seen these faces, faces baked by the sun, hardened by many winters. I have heard the same short laughter, watched the same steady eyes. I have seen them in Hupeh Province, and Yunnan; I have

seen them in Kweichow and Shansi and in the valleys of the Yangtse – I
have seen them all over China, the faces of China's 600 million peasants.

Now, one by one, they get up, stretch, give a goodbye gesture with
their hands and walk back to the fields.

What tremendous changes these peasants have seen since the days of
the old society! Then, these open fields were divided into many tiny
individual plots, more than half of them owned by a landlord who
would demand fifty or sixty per cent of the produce for rent. And those
plots which were owned by a peasant were mostly too small to support a
family, forcing them also to work for the landlord. The landlords and
money-lenders dominated the lives of the peasants. Nearly always in
debt, nearly always hungry, their lives were infinitely precarious.
Floods in the Peking area were frequent and would drive thousands
from their homes. (In the 108 years before 1949, the Yong Ding River
near the city flooded no fewer than 107 times, causing enormous dev-
astation. Peking itself is built on the silt from the Yong Ding.) With no
reserves, a bad harvest meant that thousands would be reduced to
eating bark and grass, hundreds would die. Nature has not dealt kindly
with China. Only fifteen per cent of this vast country is suitable for
cultivation. She has, in the past, suffered appallingly from natural
disasters. She has had the world's worst earthquake (830,000 people
killed); the worst famine (12 million deaths); the world's greatest flood
(9,000,000 drowned); the worst landslide (200,000 killed).

The conditions of the peasants prior to 1949 – even those living
here, near Peking – had changed little throughout the centuries.
Indeed, they lived in much the same way as peasants had lived 2,000
years before – in the same poverty, the same ignorance and superstition.

From time immemorial China's peasants had struggled to improve
their conditions. Throughout China's history there were constant peasant uprisings. Peasants in other countries are usually the most conserva-
tive force, resisting change. Not so in China. The Chinese peasantry
had a long history of rebellion. Their conditions were so wretched that
they knew that *any* change would be an improvement.

Thus, it was the peasants – men and women such as I was now
meeting in the Peking Communes – whom Mao Tsetung and the
Communist Party appealed to, and organized. Long before their final
victory in 1949, Mao Tsetung had expressed his passionate faith in the
peasants and his certainty that they would form the spearhead of the
Revolution and provide its massive thrust. 'Several hundred million

79

peasants,' he wrote in 1927, '... will rise like a tornado or tempest ... They will break through all the trammels that now bind them ...'

When it came, the Revolution was indeed a hurricane and one of vast and terrifying proportions. Even here, within a few kilometres of Peking, landlords and money-lenders were placed before village meetings and put on trial for hoarding grain when people were dying of hunger, for the rape of village girls, for the extortion of the peasants' produce, for the torturing of debtors. At last the peasants could express their pent-up bitterness. In front of the very eyes of the landlords, in dramatic ritual burnings, they flung title deeds and debtors' notes into the flames. No power on earth could now control the vast accumulated anger of the peasants. Some landlords (who knows how many?) were summarily executed; many more were deprived of their possessions and made to work and live as ordinary peasants.

Thus a system of land-ownership that had survived every attempt at reform for 2,000 years was utterly destroyed. The old social order was dead. Power had passed from the land-owning classes into the hands of the peasants.

Land reform, the division of the land among the peasants that followed the overthrow of the landlords, honoured the revolutionary promise 'land to the tiller!' and it fulfilled the deep longing of every peasant to own his own piece of soil. The peasants were no longer forced to give up half or more of their produce for rent. They were no longer in debt. They were no longer in fear. 'It was,' one old peasant said, 'as if a big rock had been lifted off my back.' But the division of land was only the beginning of many new struggles and difficulties. True, the peasants possessed their own land, but the plots were still inadequate and certainly provided no base for agricultural development. Food was still scarce. Men and women were still harnessed like animals to pull their wooden ploughs. Irrigation was urgently needed. There were around Peking a few scattered wells operated with hand winches, and on the former landlords' estates there were pumps operated by donkeys. But there was not a single reservoir. There were no deep wells, no electricity, no pumping stations; and the Yong Ding River still overflowed its banks in the rainy season. The way out for agriculture was clearly larger fields and mechanization, but in the whole of the Peking area there were only two worn-out, foreign-made tractors.

Out of the sheer logic of this situation the peasants began to form what they called 'Mutual Aid' teams. Six to a dozen households who had adjoining land found that it paid to lend each other tools and help each other when the work was hard. These Mutual Aid teams were the beginning, the start, the first seed, from which future collectivization would grow and which, in a few years, was to transform the whole of China's agriculture.

The government supported these efforts and urged the peasants to widen their collaborative efforts. GET ORGANIZED! was one of the slogans of the time. So, between 1952 and 1954, groups of these Mutual Aid teams began to form voluntary co-operatives in which land, animals, tools and labour were shared. Eventually these developed further and everything except the peasants' houses and the land immediately surrounding them, was not only shared but communally owned. When I was in China in 1957, these 'Advanced Co-operatives' had spread virtually throughout the entire country.

The Advanced Co-operatives represented a long stride forward from the first minuscule, individually owned plots, but they turned out to be only the jumping-off stage for a still greater and more far-reaching development – the formation in 1958 of the People's Communes.

I have already mentioned 'Communes' and it is time I described what they are. But, first, it is necessary to explain what they are *not*.

A tremendous outcry occurred abroad when news of the Communes first reached the West. For more than a year, even responsible newspapers printed lurid stories of hundreds of millions of men and women being herded into huge barracks, with families divided and babies torn from their mothers' arms. 'The first serious effort in history to put a whole nation on what amounts to a prison chain-gang' was how one well-known writer (who had never been to China) put it. That was one of the more charitable descriptions. The memory of these stories lingers, and the word 'Commune' for many Westerners still carries sinister undertones. Some who disbelieved these stories nevertheless concluded that the Communes must be something akin to the kibbutzim in Israel.

They are not at all like the kibbutzim, and there was never a word of truth in any of the many horror stories, as numerous respected reporters and agricultural experts have since verified. I myself travelled all over China soon after these stories appeared, visited literally hundreds of villages and never saw a single 'barrack'. Families were living in the same little houses they always had. For Communes are not 'barracks' or any other kind of structure, but new administrative areas formed when several Advanced Co-operatives combined to form still larger units. Just as in the United States or Britain, wherever you set foot you will be in a county, so wherever you might be in the Chinese countryside – though the nearest buildings might be a hundred kilometres away – you will be in a People's Commune. Thus, the many hundreds of Advanced Co-operatives within the Peking area were combined to form 272 People's Communes.

To get an idea of what life in these Communes is like and how they function, we should start with one of the innumerable small villages that surround Peking, for the village, or 'Production Team' as it is called, is the basic unit of the Commune. (I shall continue, inaccurately, to call the Teams by our more familiar term 'villages'.) The villages vary in size, but let us take one that I have visited several times. It consists of, perhaps, forty or fifty households. The low adobe cottages, many of them white-washed, lie in no fixed pattern but haphazardly with little dusty lanes between them. Some roofs are thatched, some are grey-tiled with the traditional curved roof. They are very modest, these small houses, but each has a plot of ground or garden around it enclosed by a low mud wall. If you look over some of these walls you will see a profusion of sunflowers, marigolds, geraniums, growing among the vegetables. Perhaps a fruit tree, too, and from a pen in the corner you will, more likely than not, hear the grunting of the family pig.

During a hot summer day, with the men and women off in the fields, there is little activity to be seen in the village. Hens will be pecking hopefully here and there; a grandmother, holding a little child with one hand and carrying a basket in the other, might be walking slowly back from the village store. You might see two boys bringing home bundles of small twigs – fuel with which to cook the evening meal; or a cart going by, the driver sitting sideways on the shafts and, out of habit, idly flicking his horse with a whip; and up the street a small boy doing his best to guide a duck with her row of ducklings towards the village pond. These are the kind of quiet, almost sleepy, happenings you might see at noon-time on a hot summer's day. You will see no beggars, for everyone now has work; you will see no children with running sores or swollen stomachs, for food now is plentiful and one of the houses in this village has been turned into a clinic where every child is regularly examined, and if his needs are serious he will be sent for cure to the Commune hospital. There are no rich in this village and no one is destitute; there are no masters and no servants.

The cottages, built at different times by the villagers themselves, vary in size and shape. They are owned by the families who live in them. Most of them have three small rooms and, on its own, separated from the main house, a small kitchen-room with its fireplace and chopping board, its jars of rice and pickles, and dried vegetables hanging in

Almost all peasants have a plot of ground of their own around their home.
A village shop.

Fertilizing a Commune field.

bunches from the ceiling. The privy, open to the sky, is set some distance off, to the side or back of the house.

The men and women are in the fields preparing for the harvest. Before they return, the grandmother will have cooked the evening meal of rice and vegetables and steamed buns made of dough and filled with cabbage. In the intense dry heat they will sit outside to catch what little breeze there is, and after the meal the men will sit smoking their long-stemmed pipes until darkness or tiredness sends them in. The heat does not let up at night and children, in spite of the mosquitoes, prefer to sleep out of doors.

The interiors of the houses are astonishingly similar to the workers' apartments in the city. The picture of Mao Tsetung, with many small snapshots of the family stuck into the frame; the sewing machine, the radio, the oversized wardrobe with a mirror front, a coloured enamel tray with glasses covered with a lace cloth, the inevitable thermos. They are all here. But there are differences. Here the walls are white-washed and the floor is of earth, tamped smooth and hard. The windows are latticed, often covered with paper instead of glass; and – what you would never see in a city apartment – the traditional *kang*. The *kang* is a marvellously ingenious Chinese invention. It consists of a two-metre wide enclosed brick 'box' which is used both as a table and a bed. It often runs the full length of the main room under the window – taking up much of the floor space. During the day the *kang* is covered with a thin rush-mat and used as a table, the family eating their meals on it, sitting cross-legged. At one end – again as in the worker's apartments in the city – there will be a pile of colourful and neatly folded quilts. It's in winter, however, that the *kang* comes into its own. For inside the *kang* a fire can be lit which warms the bricks so that they act as a big radiator, and as it is wide enough for several members of the family to sleep on, it will warm them too, at night. I wonder how many centuries ago some-one first thought up the idea!

Some might wonder what the peasants do in winter, for Peking has a cold climate and for several months the land is frozen hard. In former times there was no winter work, which only added to the hardship. That is now quite changed. Today, with thick padded coats and fur-lined hats with flaps over the ears, the peasants are almost as busy in winter as in the spring and summer. There is terracing to be done and new houses built; rice seedlings must be planted in the hot-houses to be ready for the first planting; ice blocks must be cut in the river, wrapped in matting and buried, ready for the Peking markets when the warm weather arrives; if the frost level is not too deep, fields can be levelled and drainage pipes laid; new wells can be dug and power lines run to pumping stations. The school may need a new room or the rice-drying ground may require resurfacing; new orchards can be prepared and the small workshop or the Commune factories can often use more hands.

I have described a village at some length, for these small communities – and there are over 4 million of them in China – form the base on which Chinese agricultural developments have been built. I remember how surprised I was at the extent to which these Production Teams manage their own affairs. The people elect their own leaders, and they, in turn, make the routine day-to-day decisions – which fields should be cultivated, who will be detailed to look after the ducks, or clear an irrigation ditch or terrace a hill. If anything of more importance comes up a full Team meeting is called. I have, at different times, been to several such meetings. They are open to everyone – there may be mothers with babies in their arms, old men, young Communist Party stalwarts, even children come to listen. I have heard angry complaints of the village leadership being aired at these meetings, but usually discussions are about less volatile concerns – whether or not they can afford to take labour off the fields to build a maternity room at the village clinic; whether a further allocation from the Welfare Fund should be made to the Old People's Home; or, more simply, a discussion of the next season's production plans.

Perhaps the most important are the annual meetings, usually held after the harvest is in, when the Team's budget is decided. How is their produce and cash income to be allocated after making a deduction (usually between five and seven per cent) for the state tax? How is the grain to be divided after they have sold their basic norm to the state? How much *additional* grain above their norm should they sell to the state for a higher price, and how much should be put into the Team's grain reserves? How much cash should be placed in the Welfare Fund to maintain the Old People's Home for those who have no family to look after them, and to meet unexpected cases of need? These discussions involve the intimate structure of the community and the very livelihood of the people, for their decisions will, in the end, determine how much money and how much grain will be left over for the people themselves.

What do Peking's agricultural workers finally end up with for themselves when these various allocations have been made? It varies, of course, according to the harvest, to the amount the village earns by 'side occupations' such as raising ducks and fish, the products of their workshops, and so on. In actual cash the returns by our standards are almost unbelievably small, lower even than those working in the city factories. (Their expenses, of course, are lower too.) What an individual actually accumulates during the year are work-points earned by the amount of work he has put in. The quality of the work and personal attitudes are also taken into account, and whether the work is heavy or light. These work-points are then translated into cash and grain when the accounts are made up.

Until recently, each group of workers in the fields would appoint one of their number to go to a book-keeper at the end of a day to have the number of hours each member had worked recorded. Now in an increasing number of teams the members work out and declare their own workpoints at the end of the accounting period, perhaps every six months, and the figure each family puts forward is then discussed. 'Self appraisal, public discussion', the peasants call it. This, of course, eliminates the book-keeping work – but it also demonstrates the degree of trust that exists between the members of these Teams. It only rarely happens, I was told, that a member's assessment of the time he has worked is disputed.

Figures vary from Team to Team, but it usually works out that the individual worker will get somewhere between ¥1 and ¥1·5 (32–48p, 60–90¢) a day, and a more-than-usable kilo of grain distribution per day for each member of his family. This means that almost all families now have sizeable *family* reserves of grain in addition to the larger collective reserves. Low as the cash income is, there is hardly a family that doesn't have at least one bicycle, the majority have a sewing machine and – perhaps, most astonishing of all – almost every family has some savings in a bank.

The financial resources or manpower of a Team, of forty or fifty households, are, of course, very limited. To buy a tractor, for example, would be utterly beyond them, and even to dig an irrigation ditch might take too many workers from the fields. So ten or twelve – sometimes more – of the Production Teams join together in a larger association known as 'Production Brigades'. There are projects, however, that even these Brigades cannot tackle on their own – the construction of a small fertilizer factory, the building of a reservoir, the establishment of a modern, well-equipped hospital or a more advanced educational system, the building of roads, the allocation of funds for agricultural research – all needed, but all too big to be tackled by a single Brigade. So fifteen, or twenty (and in some cases over a hundred) Production Brigades work jointly, and it is these associations of Brigades that are known as the 'People's Communes'. As I have mentioned, there are

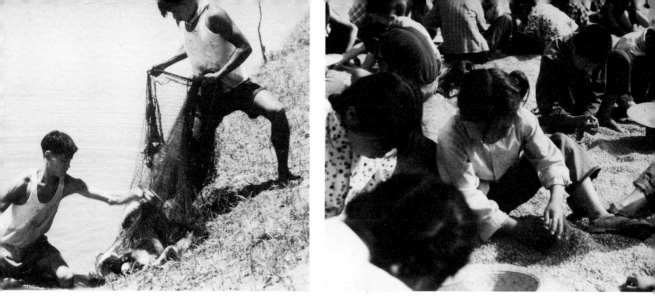

Left, a Commune fish-breeding pond. *Right*, in Peking even small children help at harvest time. Here they are busy cleaning the rice grain in a drying yard.

The entire village helps to bring in the grain.

272 Communes in Greater Peking and 50,000 Communes in all of China.

This three-tier system – Team, Brigade and Commune – was a brilliant agricultural innovation, on the one hand allowing small communities to live and work together and, to a large extent, run their own affairs, and on the other, enabling very large agricultural developments to be carried out.

Yet, before these Communes could be fully established, China found herself on the brink of a major agricultural calamity.

When I arrived in Peking in 1960, I realized that something was seriously wrong. Every patch of soil in the city had been planted with vegetables, even the little circles of earth around the trees. Food in the markets was short, rationing of a number of commodities had been reintroduced. There was an atmosphere of crisis. For three years there was unprecedented drought in some areas, floods in others. In one Commune I saw lines of peasants wearily carrying buckets of water to fields five kilometres away, in the hope of saving a crop that had already been replanted three times. I saw peasants coming in from the fields, tired and hungry, and all there was to eat was a single bun made of dough. No one actually died of starvation during that crisis, but for months it was touch and go.

The drought and floods were not the only cause. Another basic reason for the near calamity was that the development of industry had been too much favoured at the expense of agriculture. This complex problem faces all poor countries: You cannot industrialize a nation if the population is ill-fed and if agriculture cannot produce the raw materials that industry needs; but equally, you cannot improve agriculture without an industry that is able to supply tractors and fertilizers, insecticides, rural electrification, pumps and transport. This inter-relatedness of agriculture and industry was one of the most difficult problems that China had to solve after the Revolution, and it was here that the greatest errors were made. But the Chinese leadership learnt the lesson of the 1960–2 crisis. Mao Tsetung enunciated the principle of worker-peasant alliance. From that moment, agriculture was declared to be the 'foundation' of the Chinese economy with industry the 'leading factor'. This was a recognition that China's national economy must be based on the successful development of her agriculture. From then on a new order of priorities was established and a greater proportion of the available capital resources was devoted to the improvement of agriculture.

The reason why Peking was enlarged to include both city and country was to make Peking as far as possible a viable self-reliant community, with the rural areas able to feed the city population and the city able to supply the surrounding Communes with all they needed for their development. The facts show that this objective has now been largely achieved. In a city that possessed only two old tractors, there are now 4,000 medium and large-scale and 13,000 small tractors; 25,000 deep wells have been sunk and have been worked without lowering the basic water level below ground; twelve reservoirs have been built; the Yong Ding River has been harnessed; more than seventy per cent of all cultivated land in Greater Peking is now under irrigation, in some Communes one hundred per cent. Though the usable land area has been reduced by one-sixth due to the expansion of the city, the grain yield is now four times what it was in 1949, the gain in cotton yield, five times. With large areas of hot-houses, fresh vegetables are available in the Peking markets throughout the year. The vegetables grown in the Peking Communes – one hundred varieties in all – are now supplying all of the city's requirements and an almost equal amount is shipped to other cities. Over 65,000 hectares of orchards growing apples, pears, peaches and persimmons are more than meeting the city's needs. (Tropical fruit such as bananas and pineapples are brought up from southern China.) And nothing is wasted. Even the sewerage from the city, after treatment, is piped out to Communes for use on the fields.

The result of all this is that the people of Peking are no longer at the mercy of the climate and no longer need to improvise from harvest to harvest. Drainage and irrigation schemes allow full harvests regardless of the weather – indeed, since the 'bad years' of 1960–2 there has not been a single crop failure, in spite of droughts.

I realize that this description of Peking's Communes, how they developed and how they function, and the successes they have achieved, is over-simplified and would leave a misleading impression unless some other facts are added. The progression from land reform to the relative abundance of today did not go as smoothly as I have made it sound. Figures, however impressive, tell only half the story. They leave out the unimaginable prodigies of labour that made the achievements possible, and they leave out, too, the many human problems and the suffering that are involved in changing from one social system to another.

Take, for instance, the role of women. Ignorance and superstition did not vanish overnight simply because a family, for the first time, owned its own land. Under the Marriage Law of 1950, women were granted freedom to marry and divorce; they became entitled to equal pay for equal work; they could retain their maiden name. Polygamy, child betrothal and marriages arranged for money were made illegal. But, so opposed were many men to these new laws, and so psychologically incapable were women of throwing off the straitjacket in which they had for so long been pinioned, that this law at first had little effect. So little, in fact, that a vast educational programme was launched in 1953. Cadres – 3½ million of them – travelled from village to village urging women to make use of their new freedoms and to explain to men why it was time for some ancient customs to be turned upside down. Women's Associations were set up in almost every community, and once women began to understand and to exercise their rights, there were in many cases bitter struggles within the home. Women, intimidated by their husbands, began in great numbers to sue for divorce. It was reported that in some cases women actually committed suicide. A good many older men and women, I believe, may still resist these new ideas.

Of the Team committees which I attended around Peking, I noticed that about a third were women, but I also noticed that the men did most of the talking! Often, it was only when I directed a question specifically to a woman that she would, usually rather shyly, give a reply. The advance in the status of women – and this is true particularly in and near the cities – has been enormous. The fact that women now *legally* have all the rights that men enjoy is, in itself, a huge step forward. But it takes a long time to change deeply embedded ideas, as many women in the West have found. Even in communities close to Peking, some older people find it impossible to give up ancient superstitions and customs. I know of one family which still insists on keeping a new-born infant indoors for three months before risking its health by exposing it to the open air. I know another where the grandmother will have no mirror in a room that can be seen from the bed; and it is still fairly common for old men and women to have their coffin made and brought into the house, sometimes years before they actually die.

Behind these personal struggles there lies an even larger *political* struggle – what the Chinese call 'The Two Lines' – those who want to build a socialist state and those who still resist it; those who believe in communal ownership and those who still wish to go it alone. There are those whose instinctive response to any proposal is 'What is there in it for me?' and others who judge by the advantages it will bring to the community as a whole. There are some who believe that 'efficient management' is more important than allowing peasants and workers to solve problems at the grass roots on a do-it-yourself basis. When things go wrong, or there are organizational disagreements, those who still do

A Neighbourhood
Committee in session.

Tending Peking's many
trees.

Producing food for the city's population: *facing page*, picking tomatoes; *above*, loading trucks with fresh produce, and *below*, vegetables for sale in a street market.

Selling vegetables in a covered market.

The live poultry section of a covered market.

not accept the principle of collectivization always advocate a retreat from socialism. These struggles tend to be particularly acute in the countryside because Chinese agriculture, in spite of its recent almost unbelievable success in enlarging production, is not as advanced economically or socially as industry. The wages of an industrial worker in the city do not depend on the success or otherwise of his particular factory, for wage standards are the same all over the country. The agricultural worker's return for his labour varies according to the productivity of his Commune, Brigade or Team – and this will vary from one area to another, depending on whether or not there is good soil and good leadership. This inequality is the reason for the Chinese considering agriculture to be still in a backward state. It has, however, succeeded, for the first time in China's long history, in lifting the fear of starvation from her people – one-fifth of the human race.

Two memories of my travels in 'rural Peking' stand out with particular vividness. One is the wheat harvest. For days we had been watching the wheat as it turned from green to gold to deeper gold. Among the agricultural workers and the cadres there was a growing sense of moving towards an enormous 'event', the climax of months of effort, of sowing, irrigation, careful cultivation. There was an element of crisis too, for the climate around Peking is such that the period between the moment when the wheat is ripe for cutting and the first rains is very brief. If the harvest were started just a day or two too late, thousands of tonnes of wheat would be lost. There were many anxious discussions between the leaders of the Communes and the Peking meteorological office in those last days.

In the city, too, schools, shops, factories, government offices, were making *their* preparations, for they would be sending contingents out to the fields in rotation to help the workers bring in the harvest in time.

When the signal came to start, everything was in readiness. Great combine harvesters that had been repaired and greased began to move back and forth across the wheat fields while hundreds of workers followed, piling sacks of grain on to trucks and wagons. In most fields the work was done by hand. It was a great sight – college students, high-school boys and girls, learned, bespectacled men and women from the Ministry of Culture, senior officials from the Ministry of Foreign Affairs, workers from offices and factories, typists and bank assistants, managers and apprentices – all out there in the blazing sun with their sickles, or tying up the sheaves, and stacking them in rows – an extraordinary communal effort of the city Peking and the rural Peking.

In the city itself, every open space was being used for the drying of the wheat after it had been threshed. In one area we noticed that the P.L.A., the army lads, were helping to sack, weigh and record the wheat that had been brought in on carts. The little primary school children were not left out either, for in the open space in front of the city stadium we saw hundreds of these youngsters having a fine old time cleaning the dried wheat, sifting it through their small fingers, removing any bits of straw or small stones. We were in the Western Hills during these days, and there also we found whole stretches of roadway covered with the drying wheat. That took first priority and cars were detoured across the bumpy verge.

Two days after the last wheat was in, dried, sacked and in storage, the rains came down!

The other experience that remains vividly in my memory is a visit we paid to the Double Bridge People's Commune which lies about thirty kilometres to the east of Peking's central district. This was not to be the usual camera-and-note-taking expedition. A little explanation is needed to make clear why this was a special occasion.

Several hundred Chinese students of college age or older have been sent at regular intervals to various countries abroad for specialist study or to improve their foreign language. As an experiment, the Chinese government sent a few *young* children abroad both to learn the language fluently and to begin to understand Western customs and ways of thinking. Four or five were sent to Germany, the United States, France and other countries, and two were sent to Britain.

Thus it was that one afternoon two wide-eyed Chinese children were brought to our home in London to become for several years members of our family. The boy, Hung Hsing, was ten; the girl, Han Kuo-hung, was twelve. (They did, indeed, become very much a part of our family!)

This explains why on that morning Elena and I set out from Peking with great eagerness, for we were to meet Kuo-hung's family and see for the first time where our 'adopted daughter' was born and brought up before she was chosen to be one of those to be flown off to a distant country.

We met the leader of the Double Bridge Commune at the Commune headquarters and after giving us tea, he guided us to the village where the Han family lives. It is a small village, very much the same as all the others. We passed the clinic; then the village school where lots of brightly dressed children (as children always are in China) were out playing hopscotch and skipping, Chinese style, with intricate variations, not using a rope but a string of rubber bands. Then on to Kuo-hung's house – and there in the road were the family waiting to greet us.

The Han family: *above*, the family at table; 1 father, a waggoner; 2 mother in her outside kitchen; 3 younger daughter at primary school; 4 elder son, just returned from the P.L.A.; 5 younger son working in the fields; 6 Kuo-hung (in Regent's Park in London).

4

6

And what a greeting it was! Father, mother, older sisters, younger sister, brothers, grandchild, brother-in-law, sister-in-law, the family dog, the cat – they were all there. Handshakes and laughter – we felt surrounded by excitement and affection. 'Our daughter is a member of your family,' said the mother, 'so you are both members of ours! Come along, come inside!' And taking us both by the hand, she led us through the garden gate, through the little yard and into the house. How we all managed to squeeze in I don't know, for our friends Lü and Yu Ma were with us and Chung Ho-shan, the Commune leader, and the drivers of the cars and several others.

Taking our shoes off, Elena and I sat cross-legged on the brick *kang* with Kuo-hung's father and mother on either side of us. We talked, and our interpreters had difficulty in keeping up, for there were so many questions to be asked and answered. We described as best we could the kind of life that Kuo-hung was leading in London, how she had adjusted to such different conditions, the school she was going to, how fluent her English was becoming and what wonderful Chinese meals she sometimes cooked for us. They laughed and asked more questions and then in turn told us what she was like as a little girl.

'She writes to us happily,' they said.

'Yes, but she misses you all terribly, and her friends, and the village ... and China.'

'We miss her too,' they said, 'but that is unimportant, for when she comes back she will be able to help our country.'

And this was said with great simplicity and conviction.

Two older sisters had slipped out to the kitchen in the yard and now they were back carrying dish after dish of food. Vegetables from their garden, fish from the pond behind the house, chicken (we learned later that they had killed their two roosters for the occasion), rice, steamed buns, noodles and many other dishes. As we ate we asked about the different members of the family. The father is a waggoner driving one of the Team's horse carts; a son was just back from three years in the army and was helping in the fields until he was assigned to some technical work in the city; two daughters are teachers; the younger daughter is still at the village primary school; a brother-in-law was working as a physicist at the atomic research station in Peking. The father told us about his life in former years, when he worked for a landlord. His early years were years of deprivation and hardship. They had left their mark, for he looked twenty years older than his age. But there was great humour in his wrinkled face and he turned away from the story of his youth with a laugh. The mother, with her high cheekbones and a refined appearance was watching us all with very calm eyes. I felt that it was she who kept the family together and had seen it through bad times. There was no anxiety in her face – rather an unusual serenity.

After we had eaten, Elena suggested that we write a letter to Kuo-hung in London which we could all sign, and the mother dictated it to one of the sons. When I handed her the pen to sign her name she said, 'I cannot read or write – except my name.' Very slowly and carefully she wrote the characters, and the father did the same.

We sat for a while sipping tea. How utterly remote London seemed from this small Chinese village. Another world. What enormous differences there were between the life experience of this family and our own. Yet here we were comfortable and at ease with each other. This family, I thought, represented what was happening all over China – mother and father illiterate, their children becoming teachers and doctors, physicists and engineers, pilots and poets. And Kuo-hung herself, probably at this moment struggling to make sense of the kings and queens of England, or the 'new maths', or Chaucer or the Greek myths! Perhaps she represents the China of the future, whose people will one day intermingle freely with the rest of mankind.

It was time for us to leave; after taking photographs we made our way to the cars. The family all came out to the little road to see us off, and a crowd of village children too. During the many goodbyes and promises to return, the mother handed Elena a huge bag of peanuts 'For all you are doing for our daughter.' Then we were on our way. They kept waving and we kept waving until the dust hid them from view.

6 *Who Runs Peking?*

In the government of a city, or a nation, one question inevitably arises. In the words of Engels, 'How can you prevent those who should be the servants of society from acting as its masters?'

Certain officials sitting behind their desks have been given the responsibility to see that the administration of their city proceeds in a smooth and orderly way. The streets must be cleaned, the garbage must be collected, schools must be provided, stray dogs must be caught, broken water-pipes must be repaired ... the list of their duties is varied and endless. Every day public officials make so many decisions, issue so many regulations 'on behalf of the people', that they soon believe that they know what is good for the man in the street better than he knows it himself. The longer they remain behind their departmental desks deciding this and regulating that, the less do they feel like servants. This is a universal hazard.

In Peking, the Cultural Revolution, which churned up everything, brought the problem of the city's bureaucracy to the surface. For months the people of Peking debated this question, as they did everything else. I happened to be in Peking in 1967 when the old guard who had run the city were finally overthrown and the first 'Peking Municipal Revolutionary Committee' was elected. The people had ousted an entrenched bureaucracy and, judging by the jubilation, they must have had a hard but worthwhile struggle. The victory was celebrated with enormous noise as the people marched in a hundred unorganized processions with drums and clashing cymbals. Fireworks and dancing in the streets went on until late into the night. It was an exciting day.

So in 1967 the people threw out the old lot and elected a new. Has it been working any better than the old? The citizens of Peking believe that they have devised a system which will make officials more responsive to the needs of the people, and act more to serve than control. Perhaps, even now, it is too early to tell whether they have succeeded or not. But before we consider how the people approach the problem of

96

bureaucracy it might be useful to see in outline the structure of the city's administration.

PEKING REVOLUTIONARY MUNICIPAL COMMITTEE

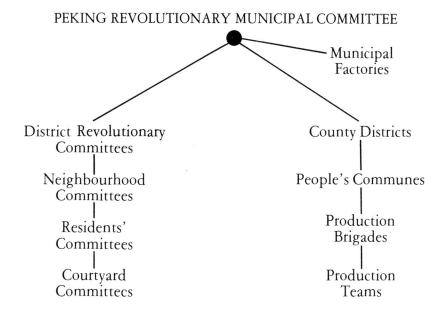

A District Revolutionary Committee

To understand how the urban five-tier structure works in practice, we first visited the 'Western District Revolutionary Committee', one of Peking's four urban District Committees. (A District Committee in Peking is roughly equivalent to the Westminster City Council in London, or the Manhattan Borough Council in New York.)

The Committee was already in session when we arrived. They were expecting us, and the Chairman introduced us to members of the Committee. During these preliminaries I asked whether I could take some photographs and they agreed I could. The Committee members then settled back to continue their business.

This is the description I scribbled in my notebook:

Fourteen or fifteen sitting on each side of a long table which is covered with a green-patterned plastic cloth. Only four women. The Chairman – a somewhat stocky figure with a serious face that occasionally breaks into a broad smile. He has a down-to-earth appearance. He chain smokes like several others – none of the women are smoking at all. General atmosphere of the meeting is relaxed but the discussion is business-like. Decisions are made and recorded, then the next matter is taken up. No long flights of oratory. No one interrupts a speaker with questions or comments – they come when he or she has finished. The others actually *listen* to whoever is speaking, they don't just wait for a chance to push in with their ideas. I wish we could run committee meetings this way.

It was late when the Committee meeting broke up, too late for us to ask questions. So Elena and I, with our two Chinese companions, returned another day. We met the Chairman in his small and rather sparsely-furnished office. After a few minutes the woman Vice-Chairman joined us. From them we gained the following information.

The area of Peking under the Western District Committee is almost thirty square kilometres, with a population of 660,000. The Committee consists of thirty-three members, twelve of whom are women. Sixteen members are elected by the District cadres as their representatives. The other seventeen are elected every two years by the people of the District through their Neighbourhood Committees (see chart). Among these seventeen, eight are factory workers, three are shop assistants, one is a doctor, one a teacher, two are policemen, one is a bus-ticket collector. Six of the members are young, and by 'young' they said they meant 'under thirty'.

Working under the District Committee there are 233 officials and office staff (which is 200 less than before the Cultural Revolution). This struck me as being an astonishingly small number considering the range and variety of the activities for which the Committee is responsible. The work is divided into Departments – Industry, Communications, Construction, City Planning, Culture and Education, Commerce and Trade. Under the overall jurisdiction of the District Committee there are seventy-eight factories (the larger factories are under the Municipal Committee), 2,100 shops (with 30,000 shop assistants), 71 middle schools (with 110,000 students and 7,700 teachers), 98 primary schools (with 66,000 students and 4,600 teachers). The District Committee is responsible for 7 cinemas, 3 workers' clubs, 3 hospitals and 11 out-patient clinics and a district library.

It was at this point that I remembered Engels. I asked the Chairman what was to prevent the city officials – and the members of the Revolutionary Committee itself – from gradually coming to think of themselves as the masters and not the servants of the people. He said:

Since the Cultural Revolution we have been practising the 'three-three' system. We think that this is a safeguard against the dangers you have mentioned. Under this system only one-third of the officials remain at any one time in their offices attending to the normal running of the District. They see to the countless matters that constantly arise in a big city.

Another third are engaged in what we call 'social investigation' at the grass-roots level. They move around the District, talk to the people, learn their problems and wherever possible solve the problems on the spot. They investigate complaints, see that the public services are being properly carried out ...

What kind of complaints?

Almost anything you can think of. Perhaps in one of our streets the garbage isn't being collected regularly; there may be a complaint about the bus service which we can look into and pass on to the Municipal authority concerned. They will also investigate where new housing is most urgently needed, or a new out-patient clinic, or where a policeman should be posted to help children cross the street when school lets them out – things like that. We believe that with one-third of the cadres looking into matters of this kind we can keep closely in touch with the needs of the people in our District. We are also helped by the many suggestions that come to us from the people. We follow up these on the spot to see whether or not we can put them into effect. We used to decide these matters in the office – now we actually investigate them. I should also add that any official, or any of us on the Committee, can be recalled if the people think we are not doing a good job!

And the last third?

They take part in some form of manual labour – in a factory perhaps or in one of the many May 7th Cadre Schools [described later] that have been set up near the city, and they undertake political study as well. So of the officials administering this District, one-third are in the office, one-third are investigating at the grass roots level and one-third are doing manual work and political study. Then, every six months – though this may vary in individual cases – they rotate their work. We believe that this system guarantees organizationally that the officials and staff will not begin to think of themselves as superior beings alienated from the people, will not forget what it is to do manual work, and will not lose sight of one of our basic political objectives which is to be of service to the people.

What about the Committee members themselves?

Oh, we follow the same system. Our full Committee meets only once every four months but we have a standing (or executive) committee of ten, who meet every week. But as some of the Standing Committee will be studying conditions at the grass-roots level and others will be doing manual work, there are times when only four members are left. The meeting you attended a few days ago was an enlarged Standing Committee meeting.

Much of the local work is now undertaken by Neighbourhood Committees – there are nine of them in our District. At an even more local level there are the Residents' Committees. Residents' Committees are not a part of the formal structure of the city administration but they are important. You might say that since the Cultural Revolution we have greatly *decentralized* the government of Peking – giving more and more responsibility to small neighbourhood units.

It sounded to me as if Peking was becoming (like so much else in China) a 'do-it-yourself' city.

May 7th Cadre Schools ... Neighbourhood Committees ... Residents' Committees ... Quite clearly, if we were to understand how Peking was run we needed to see these too.

Neighbourhood Committees

During the next few days we visited two Neighbourhood Committees in different parts of Peking. Each of them had between 50,000 and 60,000 inhabitants within their areas; both were described as 'middle-sized'.

Neighbourhood Committees are the basic unit of the formal structure of the Peking City administration. They are financed by their District Committees and though they only have a small staff, it is through these Neighbourhood Committees that the District Committee channels much of the administration. This explains the very small number of officials who operate at the District level. Many of the schools, shops, local factories, workshops and clinics are supervised by the Neighbourhood Committees though the final responsibility rests with the District. They cover a much smaller area, of course. One of the Neighbourhood Committees we visited, for example, covers only 1·5 square kilometres and consists of two main streets and 132 *hutungs*.

For many years Neighbourhood Committees throughout Peking

Above, all the main streets in Peking are washed down at night. *Above right*, Peking's new underground railway. *Right*, a retired doctor continues to work voluntarily a few days a week at a neighbourhood clinic. *Below right*, a District Revolutionary Committee in session. *Below*, a neighbourhood 'Sewing Service Shop' where people can bring their clothes to be repaired.

have been encouraging housewives and others who have time on their hands, to set up small-scale workshops. We went to a number of these. They vary greatly in size and in the products they make. They are voluntary, so only those who enjoy doing something besides their daily chores (and like a little extra cash) take part. No need to sit at home alone waiting for the children to get back from school. To join with others for some hours a day in some useful work gives the women – and sometimes older, retired men, too – a sense of contributing to the whole national effort.

Most of the workshops started in a small and somewhat amateurish way. For example, there was one which was set up before the Cultural Revolution by six women. They went to their nearest hospital and asked what they could make that the hospital needed. They were quite unskilled, for they had never worked before. The hospital gave them the equipment to make and bottle two simple liquid antiseptics. They found an unused shed which they patched up; they arranged to have water piped in, borrowed a couple of trestle tables and set to work. After the Cultural Revolution this little enterprise developed rapidly. Today it has become a small-scale but well-equipped pharmaceutical factory employing 280 people (eighty per cent of whom are women) and they are making seventy kinds of medicines. Of the original six who started this back-street workshop, three are still there helping to run it. Though not related, they happen to have the same last name, 'Lan', and they are known as 'the three Lans'.

Some of these small workshops we visited were making components for a nearby factory – assembling transistors for example for a radio factory. We saw six or seven women in a single room making dolls for a children's store. At another, a group were making wooden boxes which required little skill, while at another workshop housewives were assembling the most delicate instruments. Taken individually, a neighbourhood workshop might not add much to the overall productivity of the nation, but together (there are at least 10 million of them in China) they have a sizeable economic significance. They help to bridge the gap between an individual doing his or her own handicraft and modern mechanized production. But their greatest value, I believe, is a social value. We were often told by women in these workshops that before they began working they felt they were rather useless individuals who would never be able to understand anything mechanical. (This feeling was, of course, partly inherited from the old society where husbands would never have allowed their wives to do anything outside the house.) The workshops have given millions of women a new kind of

self-confidence, particularly in a society where people think of themselves primarily as *producers* rather than *consumers*.

Another activity which the Peking Neighbourhood Committees
help to organize is the annual city 'spring cleaning'. Every year during
May and June the whole city population is mobilized to eradicate the
sources of flies and mosquitoes. Any corner or crevice or pile of rubbish
that might be a breeding ground for flies is cleaned up; any standing
water where mosquitoes could lay their eggs is drained. The result is
that one almost never sees a fly or hears the buzzing of a mosquito in the
city. The medical people put down the low incidence of intestinal
illnesses to the virtual elimination of the common fly.

But, despite their name, even the Neighbourhood Committees are
not able to meet many of the more personal needs of the people. With
50,000 or 60,000 people in their areas, they have too many administrative duties to know the needs of individual families. So, under each of
the Neighbourhood Committees, there are thirty, forty or fifty smaller
units known as 'Residents' Committees'. These are self-governing and
are run by volunteers without pay, except for two or three medical
workers in the health clinics. These Residents' Committees are not part
of the formal structure of the city government but they play an extra-
ordinarily important part in the lives of the Peking people.

A Residents' Committee

The Committee we visited was known as the 'Brick Tower' Residents'
Committee. Now, at last, we felt we were getting close to the 'grass
roots'. The headquarters of this Residents' Committee was in one of the
old Peking houses built around a courtyard. We were met at the
entrance by Mr Liu Ru-chen, the Chairman. The Committee members
had not yet arrived so Mr Liu took us into a room and gave us tea. He
smiled gently across the tea-cups. He was clearly waiting for a cue from
us. 'Please tell us about your Committee and what it does,' I said.

> We are here to be of service to the people in this small section of
> Peking. [Then came the inevitable, but useful, statistics.] In our
> Residents' area there are 812 households, less than 3,000 people.
> Sixteen hundred are workers; 760 are schoolchildren and 260 go
> to nursery schools or kindergartens. We have 70 retired workers
> who are still active and 200 people who are too old to work. Most
> of the people have lived in this area most of their lives, so we all
> know each other quite well.

103

We have many activities. We run a clinic with two medical workers – they are paid by the District Committee. A retired doctor who lives in this area also works there for several hours a day. He receives his old-age pension, so he contributes his services without pay. The clinic gives advice to women about birth control, has an immunization programme for the children and arranges lectures on public hygiene.

Many women who are working, especially if they have several children, have almost no time for mending or cleaning clothes or altering them to fit the younger children. On the other hand, we have a number of women who enjoy sewing and would like to be of help. So we have set up a 'mending clothes' Service Shop and to this people can bring clothes that need attention. A retired tailor works there too. The charges are very modest. We have several other Service Shops – a 'mending bicycles' shop, a shop where pots and pans can be repaired, and another one for radios. An older man who, until he retired, was a worker in a watch factory has set up a 'mending watches' Service Shop. In this way retired workers feel they are still of use and part of the community.

We pay especial attention to old people. If they live alone and find walking difficult, our Committee arranges for their groceries and coal to be taken to them. If they are bedridden, we arrange with neighbours to bring them food. Old people shouldn't be left alone too much, so children on their way back from school will look in on these old people and will read the newspaper to them if they can no longer see. The schoolchildren also help to tidy up their rooms or clean up their yard.

Our Committee also, of course, arranges political study groups. We hold meetings to discuss what is going on in our country and abroad. We arrange for speakers from the city political education department to talk to us and the old people sometimes give talks to the young children to describe what conditions were like before the Revolution.

Was your Committee elected?

Yes, by the people in our area.

I noticed that the Chairman was glancing from time to time out of the window. 'I see that the other members of the Committee have arrived. As it's a warm day we shall be meeting out of doors.' He smiled. 'You can join us if you wish. We have no secrets.'

The other members were already assembled and were waiting for Mr

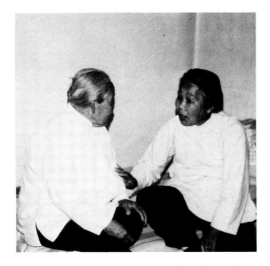

Old people who have no family to live with are looked after in homes sometimes called 'Homes for the Honouring of the Aged'. They are provided with everything they need, including visits by doctors. Young children regularly go in after school to see the old people; read to them if they cannot read; help them tidy their rooms; take them for walks, and in many other ways make the old people feel that they are still part of normal life. These old people's homes are by no means gloomy places.

Liu. The flowers in the courtyard were in bloom and the trellised vine was already in leaf. Some of the Committee were sitting on the brick steps, some on low stools. About twenty in all. They spanned several age groups. A few were old and dressed in the dark jackets that old people in China traditionally wear. Some of the younger girls were wearing coloured blouses. They waved a welcome to us. I pointed to my camera with a look that said, 'May I?' and they nodded quite happily.

We remained a short time and then reluctantly had to leave for another appointment. This group of neighbours discussing their common affairs reminded me strongly of some of the village meetings I had been to in the countryside.

Mr Liu, when he saw we were ready to leave, courteously accompanied us to the courtyard entrance. I commented on the sense of local community which still seemed so alive in Peking. We were in for one more mild surprise. 'These Residents' Committees are not the smallest groups in our city. People who share courtyards such as this have formed what they call "Face the Sun" courtyard groups. You should visit one.'

'Face the Sun' Courtyard Committees

These are a relatively new development.

Many families in Peking still live in the old single-storey houses built in the traditional manner. They are usually arranged in a series of square or rectangular courtyards, one courtyard leading into a second or even a third. Around each courtyard are small brick-and-tile rooms. Formerly, a single wealthy family would occupy one of these courtyard houses; now a few families will share it. On the other hand, the new multi-storey buildings for factory and office workers might house hundreds of families, but even these are built with wide play-areas between.

The residents in these courtyards – whether they are the old small ones or the larger play-area courts – have now organized 'Face the Sun' Courtyard Committees. (Some have called theirs by the less poetic name 'Socialist Courtyard Committees'.) The movement began when several families sharing one of the old-style courtyard houses in the north-eastern part of Peking elected a 'courtyard management committee'. The idea soon spread even to the new, larger blocks of flats.

These committees include workers, housewives, officials, even schoolchildren. They arrange for the cleaning-up of the courtyard; the children organize after-school games. Some married couples are still at work when their children return from school. Now the Courtyard Committee sees that the children have things to do until their parents return. Political discussions are also arranged, and this pleases the old ones as they can now attend without having to travel elsewhere. All kinds of arrangements are made by these Committees – baby-sitting; outings by bus; volley-ball matches against other courtyards; volunteer teams for sweeping up the leaves or planting flowers; and when it snows *everyone*, except the very old, pitches in to clear the paths.

After 1949, when land was distributed to the peasants, the first small movement towards collectivization began with 'mutual aid' when peasants would give each other a hand during the busy season. 'Mutual Aid' since then has remained deep in the consciousness of the Chinese people. If 'Serve the People' is one of the main principles that keeps Peking ticking over, then 'Mutual Aid' certainly is another.

106

Drying rice noodles.

Delivering ice which has been
stored underground since winter.

Celebrating 'Children's Day', June 1st.

Everyday activities at primary school: children at lessons, and dressed for dance and drama classes.

May 7th Cadre Schools

We left until last what must be one of the most remarkable social innovations that emerged from the Cultural Revolution, the establishment of 'May 7th Cadre Schools'. The name derives from a directive by Mao – it was dated May 7th, 1966 – in which he said that everyone, including all officials (or cadres as the Chinese call them) should learn new skills in addition to their normal work, and especially that everyone should engage in manual work of some kind and take part in political study.

Mao Tsetung was convinced that one of the reasons why socialism in the Soviet Union ceased to be socialist in character and spirit; why it developed into a rigid form of state-capitalism with a privileged class of bureaucrats, and why abroad the Soviet Union became a 'social-imperialist power' was because *political education* was largely abandoned. Mao was ever-conscious that China might go the same way. That is why he always placed the greatest emphasis on the need (especially for those in any official position) to study and really grasp the essence of Marxism-Leninism, not only intellectually but to become aware in their own lives of how relentlessly old habits of class and privilege will re-assert themselves.

Mao also believed that one way to prevent the emergence of a privileged class of bureaucrats was through manual labour. 'All evil things in the world', he once said, 'start from the divorce from labour.' But it must be labour combined with political study.

Though Mao enunciated his ideas about cadres getting out of doing some ordinary work in 1966, it was two years before the first May 7th Cadre School was started in a place called Liuho ('Willow River'). Mao gave it his support. He wrote, 'Going down to do manual labour gives vast numbers of cadres an excellent opportunity to study again; this should be done by all cadres except those who are old, weak, ill or disabled.' From that moment – as so often happened in China – May 7th Cadre Schools sprang up all over the country, 'like bamboo shoots after a rain in spring' as one Chinese put it. I don't have the figure of the number of such schools around Peking but there are probably many dozens.

We had heard much about these Cadre Schools and were anxious to see one, so one day we piled into a car and drove for about half an hour. Our journey ended at a collection of army-type barracks set on flat and rather desolate terrain. This was the school. It was during work hours and there were few people around. The school Principal came out to

107

greet us and led us to one of the huts which he said was the library and, sure enough, at one end of the room the walls were lined with books. At the other end several people rose to greet us. 'We were told that you were coming,' explained the Principal, 'so we asked these students to stay away from their work this afternoon to meet you. They can tell you about their experiences here.'

I asked if they had had many foreign visitors. 'No, you are the first,' they said. Tea was handed round and the Principal said that he would start the discussion by giving a few background facts about the school.

Since it was started in 1968, more than 4,800 students had passed through the school. Most of them stayed six months, some longer. The present generation of students numbered 320 and were nearly all from the Eastern District of Peking. The youngest student was twenty, the oldest was sixty years of age.

'There was nothing here when we first came; so the first group of students lived with the peasants in a village while they built the school. Today the students spend half the day in agricultural work, or in the kitchen preparing meals, the other half of the day is spent in political study.

'It doesn't matter what position they hold in the city, whether they are high important officials or low, whether they are teachers or factory managers, whether they are young or old — once they come here they are all workers and all equal.'

'Not quite equal,' one middle-aged man murmured under his breath and the others laughed. I looked inquiringly at the Principal. 'That's a private joke,' he said. 'We do, for some jobs, have a group or squad leader to take charge of a particular piece of work. The reason why we laughed was that this man [pointing to the man who had made the interjection] does very important work when he is in the city — he is the head of the big office that organizes all the public transportation. Soon after he arrived here he found that his squad leader was a very junior clerk in his own office!'

'Did you *mind* this?' I asked the man.

He paused. Then answered, 'Yes, I must admit I *did* mind. I had only just arrived and I felt I was being deliberately put down. The work the squad leader assigned me to was carrying manure to the field. I thought that was done deliberately too.'

'If it happened now, would you mind?'

He looked up at me and shook his head, and I believed him. Then, as an afterthought he added, 'I had been too long in an office.'

I asked the other students what they found had been their most

A May 7th Cadre School: *above left*, morning toilet; *centre*, working in the fields; *right*, picking fruit in the orchards.

Right, returning from work in the fields; *below*, cooking one's own meals; *below right*, washing one's own clothes.

useful experience at the School. A young woman answered first.

'I'm a schoolteacher. Among other things I teach biology and agriculture. One of my first jobs here was to help some peasants weed a rice-field. During the first few weeks my muscles ached and I got calluses on my hands. I didn't mind that too much. What really shook me was that when I first began to weed I, who had been teaching agriculture, couldn't tell the difference between the small rice shoots and grass, and I pulled up a lot of rice-shoots until a peasant stopped me. You should have seen the look on his face! I learned through that incident the limitations of book knowledge.'

A man spoke next. By his manner I judged him to have been accustomed to exerting authority. 'I enjoyed living in the city. My apartment is warm during the winter months. There is always good food, cooked by my wife, waiting for me when I return from the office. I can read quietly at night, or we might go out to a theatre or restaurant. I have a pleasant, comfortable life. Here, everything is different. We sleep in bunk-beds, many of us in one hut; we wash our own clothes; we take it in turns to cook in the kitchen and clean out the latrines; we eat in mess halls; we get up very early – five-thirty now that summer has come. All this took getting used to. I found it difficult and resented it at first. But now I feel fitter than I ever did in the city. [He looked very fit.] I'm *enjoying* life. I now see my life in Peking had got into a rut. I took my comforts and privileges far too much for granted. Some of the peasants around here live much harder lives even than we do here at the School.'

It dawned on me that the Principal had selected these students very carefully, perhaps so that we would be presented with a variety of experiences. A younger man spoke next:

'I am a leading cadre in a machine-tool factory. I'm one of the few who didn't mind the hard work – I was used to it. What I found difficult at first was the studying. We spend several hours every day in political study, reading or discussing some basic principle from the works of Marx, Lenin or Mao Tsetung. I felt at a great disadvantage. Many of the students here are intellectuals. They can talk better than I can. That's what I found difficult.'

'Do you still?'

'Oh no! I soon found that what they were good at was repeating what they had read in books. When I asked them, "Right – now how would you apply that to such and such a problem in a factory?" they would be stumped!' They all smiled.

I had noticed an older man who sat listening quietly, saying very little. I turned to him next.

110

'Our country,' he began, 'as Chairman Mao has said, has still far to go even before it can be properly called socialist. We still have an eight-grade pay-scale for example; we haven't eliminated bourgeois right; in many things we have nominal equality but actual inequality. These are the things we discuss together in our political sessions. In the city I'm the Secretary of a Party Committee. The *work* is important. And because the work is important I took it for granted that *I* was important. In other words, I had developed a personal outlook instead of a social outlook. This week my job is washing the dishes.' He laughed. 'You can hardly feel self-important doing work like that.'

'Go on,' I said. I felt he had more to say. I found him interesting.

'Well, to get back to the political discussions. During the Cultural Revolution some of us in the Party – including me – supported the Liu Shao-chi revisionist line. It's easy to see now that we were utterly wrong. But why didn't we see it then? How was it that even we – those of us in leading Party positions – failed to distinguish revisionist policies from Marxism-Leninism? What was it in our background or our thinking that led us to be so blind? It's *privilege*, for with privilege and "importance" it is very easy to lose one's political sensitivity. Then, when a crisis comes, one cannot distinguish clearly between two lines, one sees things subjectively, how this line or that would affect one personally. So without realizing it one chooses wrongly, as I did during the Cultural Revolution. My Party colleagues helped me to distinguish this. I didn't lose my position. But to be so blind after so many years in the Party!

'When we arrived at this school,' he went on, 'we were asked to write down what particular ideological question we wished to study while we were here. For me, because of my errors during the Cultural Revolution, the most important question is how are people to recognize revisionist thinking. This sounds so simple, but in reality it's very subtle. It can't be learned from books. It comes from one's world outlook, it has to come from inside oneself.'

I found this man's earnestness and his open acknowledgement of past mistakes strangely moving.

'One more question,' I said to the students. 'What about your families? How often do you see them? How do they manage without you?'

The young woman schoolteacher answered. 'First of all, we draw the same wages as we do when we are doing our normal work, so there's no financial hardship for our families. We have three days off every two weeks – buses take us into Peking. If our families are dependent on us for some special reason – children or an old parent in the house – neighbours are only too glad to help. We have no worries about our families, or they about us.'

The Principal then said that if we wished to see the students at their work we should go now as the afternoon was getting on. So with him we walked to the various locations where work was in progress. Some students were picking vegetables, others hoeing between rows of rice. At the piggery they were washing down the pens, and in the peach orchard they were picking the fruit.

Wherever we went we found the students working steadily and cheerfully. It's true they didn't look like peasants, but one would never have guessed that a few months earlier many of these men and women were sitting behind their desks and telephones, giving instructions, making important decisions. Bureaucracy in a different role! As I stood watching them, I had a sudden mad and glorious vision. The bureaucrats of Britain! The Establishment! The tidy, upright gentlemen from Whitehall, the headmasters of our most exclusive public schools, the chairmen of many important companies, the Directors of the Bank of England and some of our more dignified and superior politicians – I saw these gentlemen and ladies as in a great panorama, not at their desks but working for a change with their muscles on the farms and in the factories of Britain. I saw them feeding pigs and driving tractors; I saw them in the machine shops and steel works; and I saw them mucking in with workers to whom they had hardly ever spoken before. And I could feel how at first they hated it, resenting their dirty hands and aching muscles, and above all, the awful *indignity* of it; missing their comforts and the deference due to them as members of an upper class. But then, in my wild and improbable dream, I saw how first one and then another began to get the hang of the idea and begin to drop his sham importance and see himself for the first time as quite an ordinary human being... and at last, almost against his will, acknowledging that he was really having the time of his life!

My wondrous vision was interrupted by Yu Ma who said it was time for us to go. We had a last cup of tea in the library with the Principal, chatted for a while, then strolled out to the car. The work day by now was over. Some of the young men were starting a volley-ball game; others under some trees were beginning a rehearsal of a song and dance programme. We said our goodbyes and climbed into the car, and just in time a girl rushed up to us with a huge bag of peaches.

7 Feeding Peking

We have strolled through a dozen city markets, watched the teeming shoppers with their string bags; we have seen the convoys of trucks moving into Peking before dawn; we have stopped at midnight or later at one or other of the brilliantly lit all-night shops that cater for workers on the late shifts ... 'Peking, as far as vegetables, fruit and meat are concerned is self-sufficient,' we were told, 'except for tropical fruit, which comes from the south.' From out of the city to the surrounding Communes go the tractors, the electricity, the irrigation machinery, the fertilizers; and back into the city comes the food – an intricately managed reciprocal balance. 'Three and a half thousand tonnes of vegetables every day,' they said, 'enough for nearly one kilo for every baby, child and adult living in the city.'

How is it organized?

To find out we went to the Xidan market, one of the fifty or sixty 'medium-sized' markets in central Peking. It is – despite its description – a huge covered market, all on one floor. It was already jammed with shoppers when we arrived, all chattering as if they were on a spree; and with the chatter came the squawks of the ducks and geese at the live poultry department. I have never, I think, seen so much food assembled in one place, and so decoratively displayed. The fruit and vegetables, looking as if the dew was hardly off them, were stacked on sloping shelves in colourful patterns – mountains of them: cabbages, carrots, shiny purple aubergines, beans, tomatoes, cucumbers, persimmons, apples, pears. The prices seemed – to us – almost unbelievably cheap. The dressed carcasses of pigs and the mutton hung in long rows over the meat counters. There were salted foods, cooked foods to take away, live fish swimming in tanks and dead ones laid neatly side by side on great slabs of marble; at another counter, huge pyramids of wines and spirits in brightly coloured bottles ... and people everywhere: the children, and the grandmothers with babies, and men on their way home from work.

Cutting ice on the lake at the Summer Palace. It will be wrapped and stored underground to be used during summer.

As we wended our way through the crowd to the office at the back of the market, I watched these shoppers. They were sharp-eyed, especially the women. Like the French. They picked up and examined everything before they bought. There would be no chance here of passing off a wilted cabbage or setting out apples so that the bruises didn't show.

The manager invited us into his office. After serving tea he gave us a brief history of this market. It was started as an open-air market in 1917, when it consisted of about a hundred small vegetable pedlars. During the Japanese occupation it was taken over by the Japanese and served mostly their own people. After the Japanese were defeated, the Kuomintang took it over, but by that time inflation was so bad (prices sometimes changing three times in a single day) that most of the pedlars went bankrupt. When in 1949 the currency was stabilized under the new government, the market was rebuilt, enlarged and covered over. 'It is open from 7 a.m. to 7 p.m. every day including Sundays; and we have a section in the back with about the same range of goods which remains open all night.'

Looking through my notes, these are some of the questions I asked the Manager, and his replies:

How many people on average use this market?
On weekdays about 20,000 people come here every day. Sundays and holidays are busiest – on these days we often have as many as 100,000.

What foods are still rationed?
Cooking oil and grain. The cooking oil ration is still rather low – the grain ration varies according to the work that a man or woman does, but the lowest ration is 15 kilos a month for every member of the family, including infants. [Rather more than half a kilo of dry grain per head per day.] This is more than most families can use.

Presumably you pay the Communes which supply you with your produce. How much do you add on above the price you pay?
There are seasonal fluctuations, but taking the annual average for vegetables, for example, our buying cost last year was 3·4 *fen* per *jin* [a shade over 2p, 3·8¢ per kilo]. Our selling price averaged 4·1 *fen* per *jin* [or 2·6p, 4·9¢ per kilo].

Does this mark-up cover the entire cost of this market – wages, electricity, water, heating, refrigeration, etc.?
Yes, it fully covers all expenses. We do not make a profit or a loss.

Have there been any price increases in the past twenty years?
Yes, the cost of fruit has gone up sometimes, especially in bad fruit years. Otherwise the prices have remained stable or, if anything, are slightly lower. The price we pay the Communes for our produce, on the other hand, has gone up.

You say there are seasonal fluctuations. Could you give us examples?
Yes. [I shall here translate his reply into our weights and currency]. Cabbages are one-third of a pence per half kilo in summer, but 3½p, 6½¢ in the winter; tomatoes are one-third pence in summer and 19p, 36¢ per half kilo in the winter; cucumbers are 3½p, 6½¢ per half kilo in the summer and 24p, 45¢ in the winter.

The price of vegetables in the winter is coming down all the time as Communes increase their acreage of greenhouses or houses with plastic covers. They now grow 11,500 *mou* [over 800 hectares] under cover which is only six per cent of all the growing areas in the Greater Peking area – so as the area extends, the prices will come down. But even with this small percentage under glass we are able to sell fresh vegetables all the year round. One day we will be quite independent of climatic variations. But that is still a long way off.

In the warmer weather I have seen many street stalls selling vegetables and fruit. Are the prices on the stalls lower than in the markets?

No, they are the same. The stalls are set up for the people's convenience – it means that the markets are less crowded.

What per cent wastage do you have – and left-overs that go bad?

Almost none at all. The meat, and fish are kept in refrigerators; poultry, as you have seen, is sold 'live'. On some days when there is an over-abundance of vegetables we sell them very cheaply – we almost give them away – rather than let them spoil. Most of the vegetables are picked on the same day as we sell them. The trucks from the Communes start coming very early in the morning and continue to arrive at intervals all day.

How do you control the quantity and variety of the produce sent you from the country?

This is the system. Every year we make a plan with those Communes that supply this particular market. In the light of past experience we can tell them approximately what quantities and varieties we will be needing and they plant accordingly. The Communes then send us monthly reports about weather and growing conditions and whether the original plan needs to be modified. During the growing season the Communes telephone in provisional reports as to what they can supply in ten days' time, and they phone again giving more details every five days. Then every day at 5 p.m. we discuss with each Commune what amount of each item we need to have delivered the next day. In this way, by keeping closely in touch with the Communes we can balance the supply to the likely demand. Of course we make mistakes. What we try to avoid is having too much of any one item, or running short.

8 *The Children*

There is one aspect of life in Peking (and in all of China for that matter) which invariably baffles Western visitors, especially, I must add, the professional educators. There is universal agreement that the little children of China, in their wildly colourful clothing and big coloured ribbons in their hair, are adorable. But – and this is the conundrum – why don't they behave 'normally' like our children? Why don't they push each other around and squabble and fight? Why do you hardly ever hear a Chinese child whine? Why, however carefully you watch, do you hardly ever see a child clutch a toy to himself with the cry 'It's *mine*!'? When a little child is asked to come forward to recite or sing, why doesn't he or she show the slightest sign of shyness, no coy hanging back with finger in mouth, but rather steps out to give a loud and lusty rendering? How can such small creatures – I'm thinking now of those in kindergarten or primary school – dance with such precision and co-ordination? What makes them able to sit so still for so long without fidgeting? How does one get quite tiny youngsters, before their nap, to take off their shoes, jackets and sweaters and put them away neatly without any urging?

Many Westerners will jump to the conclusion that a great price must have been paid for such astonishingly 'good' behaviour, some dreadful suppression of individuality. But if that is so, why don't these children show the normal signs of tension and unhappiness? Why don't they bite their nails, suck their thumbs, wet their beds or throw the occasional temper tantrum? How (this is the central exasperating paradox) can children be both so well-behaved and at the same time appear so cheerful and spontaneous?

Are Chinese children different kinds of human beings from our own, or is it just possible that the Chinese know something about the bringing up of children that we don't know?

To find the answers, a very eminent delegation from the United States visited China. The delegation included several professors of

117

psychology, a Professor of Human Development and Family Studies, a Director of an Early Childhood Centre, a professor of sociology, a member of the National Academy of Science, and others. It was about as distinguished a group of specialists as you could find anywhere in the Western world, and for its detailed factual and statistical information their report *Childhood in China* is well worth reading.* They visited dozens of nurseries, kindergartens, primary and middle schools. They had discussions with innumerable teachers. And what, in the end, were their conclusions? This, in part, is what the editor wrote in a chapter summing up their experience:

> The outstanding feature of childhood in China and that which raises the basic problem is the high level of concentration, orderliness, and competence of the children. ... We talked a great deal to teachers about the control and restraint of children; we enquired about hyperactive and aggressive behaviour; we tried, not very successfully, to describe some of the behaviour problems in American schools. By and large, the Chinese teachers did not understand what we were talking about; they had never seen a hyperactive or disruptive child in school. Some children were occasionally 'lively' or 'naughty', but apparently not for long.

And:

> ... TWO PUZZLES... How do children learn the remarkably precise and by American standards advanced forms of dance, sculpture, and music? And how do Chinese parents and teachers manage the first signs of conflict among young children? We cannot even make a wise guess about the answers to either question and we can only testify, as others have done, to the skilfulness of five-year-old Chinese children in the performance of dance routines of memorable complexity ... The puzzle of conflict – how social restraint and amity are achieved so early and so generally – is more difficult to specify ... we left China convinced that we had seen radically different ways of thinking about and meeting children from the ways we knew as Americans.

And, earlier in the chapter:

> Over and over again we asked ourselves how the very young Chinese child was brought to competence, social grace and restraint ... how do Chinese children come to be as they are?

* *Childhood in China*, edited by William Kesson (Yale University Press, 1975).

Above, primary school children acting and singing a story.

Right, in winter *everyone* helps to clear the snow. *Below right*, Chinese acrobatics are taught in schools at an early age. *Below*, an outdoor painting class in a village school.

English is the most common language taught, but many others (including Arabic, *above left*) are also taught. *Above*, most schools have a school 'factory' where children learn some mechanical skill.

Sixty-five per cent of all children, after they leave middle school, work in the country for two years before going to college or taking up other work. *Below right*, everyday skills are also taught.

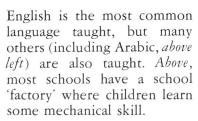

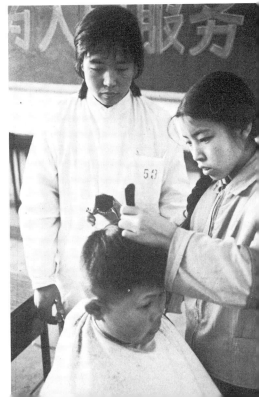

In other words, this distinguished group of American educators left China as perplexed as have so many others. Nor is it only Americans. The *Daily Telegraph* of London in a headline asked the same question: 'Chinese children: What makes them so good?'*

It is a truism that all children, not just in Peking but everywhere in the world, are conditioned by their surroundings. They quite naturally pick up the values of their parents and of the society in which they grow up. Our patterns of morality, our aspirations, our behaviour to each other, the very way we think, are all absorbed unconsciously while we are young. 'As soon as we are born,' wrote E. H. Carr, the historian, 'the world gets to work on us and transforms us from merely biological into social units. Every human being at every stage of history or pre-history is born into a society and from his earliest years is moulded by that society.'

Western children are moulded by Western competitive, individualistic values. So it is not surprising that they behave in a strikingly different way from Chinese children who have been conditioned by a society attempting to move in a wholly different direction from our own. In a 'me first' society, children will catch the 'me first' spirit. With us there is no escape from this, for in a competitive jungle a child must, for sheer economic survival later in life, learn to be self-assertive. When our children grow up it will appear to them that acquisitiveness and competitiveness are the natural order of things, that human nature is like that and (as we so often hear), *you can't change human nature!*

If the members of the delegation had studied Chinese society as a whole, its politics and social aims, they would have been less baffled by the good behaviour of Chinese children and they might have asked fewer questions about how the Chinese restrain a child's 'aggressiveness' and 'hyperactivity'.

Another cardinal distinction between Western and Chinese educational systems which foreigners sometimes lose sight of, is that in China, since the Revolution, education was designed to *change* society not (as in every other established educational system) to maintain a status quo.

A feature of education which often disturbs visitors when they arrive at a school for small children in Peking is the exuberant welcome they receive. 'Welcome uncles! Welcome aunties!' the little children chant, and as likely as not some will run forward to hold the visitor's hands. With our inveterate distrust we are sceptical of these demonstrations.

* October 18th, 1974.

'What a put-up job!' we think. (One foreign correspondent in Peking went further: 'It's horrible,' he said to me, 'the way they exploit these small children for propaganda.') These exuberant welcomings are obviously not spontaneous, but I cannot think of them as propaganda. Chinese conventions of hospitality are different from ours in a great many ways, and this happens to be one of them. If a school wishes to show that foreigners are welcome, that surely teaches the children something too. The biggest block to the understanding of the Chinese on the part of foreigners who come to Peking is the half-conscious wish, 'Why can't the Chinese be like *us*!'

We noticed that the dances and songs in the kindergartens were stereotyped and lacked what we would call individual creativity, almost as if the teachers were afraid of attempting anything original on their own initiative. The result is that you see the same dances and the same songs in every school.

A kindergarten teacher attempted to explain; or perhaps justify might be the better word.

'You must have noticed', she said, 'that there are two main themes running through many of the dances and songs we teach the children. The importance of *work* is one of them.' She was right, for we had seen that many of the songs and dances were to do with labour: 'We are carpenters on our way to build a house ...' and this they would act out with toy hammers and saws. Or they would pretend to be peasants sowing rice in the fields, or harvesting.

'We want children to grow up with a respect for work and workers, to feel that manual work is not something to look down upon but a creative part of life itself, perhaps the most important of all human activities ...'

Why the teachers could not have created their own songs and dances with this objective is another matter, but it is true, I think, that the younger people in China do have an enormous respect for peasants and workers and have no notion that there is some 'higher' status to which they ought to aspire. This attitude to work, the acceptance of it as a foremost element of life, has permeated the vast majority of the Chinese people. One might put it another way and say that a Chinese thinks of himself primarily as a producer rather than as a consumer.

'The other theme', the teacher went on to say, 'refers to our national minorities. As you know we have fifty-four different nationalities in China – almost fifty million Chinese are not ethnically the same as the Hans, but are Uighurs, Tais, Mongolians, Huis, Tibetans and so on. Before the Revolution these people were looked down on by the Hans;

Performing a Chinese minority group dance; and *below*, packing chess sets—part of practical training. These sets are sold in the Peking toy shops.

Above, paintings by children in a rural primary school, and *below right*, by a middle school pupil.

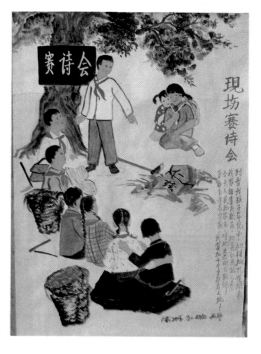

Facing page, after-school activities: middle school children playing the violin, and *below*, performing a traditional sword dance.

Peking arts: *left*, a modern dance-drama; *centre left*, figure in traditional opera; *below left*, an acrobatic group, and *right*, preparing for the famous 'lion' number.

they were among the most oppressed people in the old society.

'Even today a few still believe that the Hans are "superior" to these minority peoples. "Great Han chauvinism" we call it. It's very important that none of our children grow up with this sense of racial superiority. That is why we stress the native dances and songs belonging to these minority peoples. Our children love to dress up, say, as Mongolians and pretend to be galloping over the plains on horseback; or the girls to dress up as Tais with their long flowing dresses and slow graceful movements. We feel these early impressions are important and our children are likely to grow up with nothing but friendly feelings towards these different nationalities and think of them as part of the family of nations which make up China.'

In 1949 the new government laid down some basic principles. Education was for everyone and it was a life-time process. Education must help to eliminate the 'three great differences' – between manual and mental labour, between city and country life and between industry and agriculture. It was decided that higher education must never generate a privileged élite and that Chinese education must avoid the trend (witnessed in almost every other developing country) of encouraging a drift away from the country to the cities. 'Education for everyone' must at first have appeared an almost insuperable task. And it hasn't yet been fully achieved. Secondary and higher education, though enormously expanded, is still not available to all. Those who think that after nearly thirty years, education should by now have become as widespread as in the West might pause to consider the enormity of the problems involved when starting virtually from scratch in a country that was eighty-five per cent illiterate and where today almost half of the population of nearly 900 million is under sixteen years of age!

Let's see what *has* been accomplished.

Before 1949, there were fifteen kindergartens in Peking. They were privately run and expensive and could therefore be of use only for children of a few wealthy families.* Today in Peking there are 4,500 kindergartens and nurseries looking after 230,000 children. There are over 5,000 primary schools in Peking with nearly a million students; and 1,221 Middle Schools with an enrolment of a million and a quarter. Today in Peking every morning 2,200,000 children go off to school – more than one-quarter of the city's population.

* Before 1949 schools were run strictly as 'businesses'. They cost on average twenty to thirty silver dollars a term, which put them out of reach for the vast majority. The Chinese term for schools then was 'schooling shops' – they were selling education like a commodity.

9 Art and Culture

In Peking today there are forty-two theatres for professional actors, and seventy-two cinemas. But these represent only the tip of the iceberg. A great many factories, schools, communes and government offices have an amateur theatrical group — there are more than 9,000 of them in all. As for films there are 1,200 professional projection teams in Peking who travel from factory to factory and Commune to Commune. In three years they projected more than 100,000 shows. For those who wish to paint, there are something over 1,000 amateur painting groups and classes, and amateur photographic societies are springing up all over the city. No one has yet counted how many there are. Amateur writers, nearly all workers and peasants, also have a chance of being read. The Peking publishing house recently printed 10 million copies of books written by about a hundred spare-time writers. (An exhibition of traditional paintings in 1977 was seen by over 7 million people. In Kwanchou alone half a million people came to see this exhibition and many had to be turned away.)

Staggering figures. But what about the *content*?

To understand the cultural activities of Peking, or elsewhere in China, one must go back to the very beginnings of the revolutionary movement. The guerrilla forces then were small. To survive at all they had to persuade the peasants among whom they lived of their good intentions. The guerrillas, consisting of both men and women, wrote their own plays, formed their own dance groups, sang their own songs, not only to entertain the peasants but, more important, to convey what the Revolution was all about.

Lois Wheeler Snow in an article described how:

The Chinese revolution brought theatre to the masses. During the wars of the 1930s and 1940s out of the need to contact and educate people, and because of the centuries-old Chinese love of music and drama, theatre mushroomed wherever the revolutionaries went. Living newspapers, songs, and dance troupes, skits and

124

Left, the original painting by Hsiu Pei-hung, which has been reproduced innumerable times. *Right*, the ancient art of calligraphy is still highly honoured.

plays, even films, blossomed as actors and writers produced entertainment and educational propaganda for, and fought side by side with, the peasants. Theatre was the revolutionaries' special contact with sceptical, illiterate, hungry people who viewed *all* armies with fear and suspicion, and had to be won over to the side of the Communists to see what their armies were struggling to do ...*

And her husband, Edgar Snow, once wrote:

When the revolutionaries occupied new areas, it was the theatre which calmed the fears of the people, which gave them rudimentary ideas of the 'Red' programme, dispersed great quantities of revolutionary thoughts, to win the people's confidence. For the huge mass of Chinese there was never any fine partition between art and propaganda — only between what is understandable in human experience and what is not.†

It was Mao Tsetung who raised the crucial question: Literature and art *for whom*? This was in May 1942, seven years before the final victory of the Revolution. Speaking at the Forum on Literature and Art at

* *China Now*, January, 1975.
† Quoted in the same article.

Yenan, he answered his own question. Culture must be for everyone and not for an élite few. He went further and said that all art is related to *class*:

> In the world today all literature and art belong to definite classes and are geared to definite political lines; there is in fact no art for art's sake, art that stands above classes, art that is detached from or independent of politics. Proletarian literature and art are part of the whole proletarian revolutionary cause ...

Though Mao enunciated the general direction that he felt art and culture in China should take, there remained for quite a long time a certain confusion of artistic aims. This is not surprising when one considers that the old style of Peking opera, for example, had been performed for 140 or 150 years, so new concepts of artistic expression were not likely to catch on immediately. For another two decades the Chinese were still using forms borrowed from abroad. In 1963 I saw *Swan Lake* beautifully performed by the Peking ballet. I remember wondering at the time what possible relevance this ballet (originally devised for the upper élite of nineteenth-century Russian society) could have for the thousands who sat watching the performance – the steel workers, the miners, the peasants, men and women who had been through the searing experience of a revolution. There was no relatedness, no conceivable correspondence that I could see, between this audience and the floating, diaphanous figures on the stage.

During the tumultuous period of the Cultural Revolution there was no aspect of artistic work that was not scrutinized and fiercely debated. Writers, artists, actors, film-makers, musicians, sculptors, were all involved in these prolonged and often agonizing attempts to shed all traditional assumptions and face the basic questions which Mao had posed twenty-five years earlier: What is art? And for whom?

The answer was the same as Mao's, in all its profound simplicity. Art must not cater for any kind of cultural élite. In a socialist country it must serve the needs of *all* the people and therefore be sufficiently varied to appeal to everyone, whatever his or her level of experience and sophistication. It must express the *aims* of the new society and must therefore be related to the daily life of the ordinary people. Thus, in China today artists and writers are urged not to stand aloof from the raw and sweaty everyday world around them but to learn 'the language of the masses' by working with them in the fields and factories and to draw their inspiration from the life experiences of the workers and peasants. One artist explained it this way: 'Workers in art and literature are like cooks.

Above right, decorative glassware made at the Peking arts and crafts factory. *Left*, traditional Chinese painting is still widely practised. *Right*, every city has its own acrobatic troupe, and Peking is no exception. *Below*, a harvest dance of the Li national minority.

If the food is not to the liking of the customer it is useless and is thrown away. If you share common feelings and thoughts with the people, then you know what they want.'

Thus art in China is not (as it is so often in the West) a vehicle for 'self expression'; nor is any form of cultural work a means of gaining fame or a lucrative career. The literature, the music, the drama and cinema of China today are not focused on any individual's personal agonies, joys and passions, except in so far as a character is a symbolic expression of the stupendous efforts that the people as a whole were (and still are) required to make in order to build for themselves a wholly new kind of society.

This does not mean that Chinese traditional forms have been abandoned. ('Let the past serve the present,' Mao said.) It is rather that the old forms have been adapted to new themes. In Peking opera, for example (the favourite of all stage presentations), many of the old gestures and conventions have been retained, but it is now peasants, workers, soldiers who dominate the story. The emperors, feudal lords, dragons, noble ladies in flowing garments, have largely been replaced by characters much closer to the living experience of the people – revolutionary armies and peasants fighting oppressive landlords, Japanese invaders, or those attempting to subvert the socialist revolution. Emphasis is placed on heroism, self-sacrifice, the breaking of the shackles of the old society, the battles against the superior forces of the Japanese and Kuomintang, the rejoicing (shown in their singing and dancing) of the minority nationalities who were formerly among the most despised and oppressed of the Chinese people. Almost every drama is enlivened by the superb Chinese acrobats, battles and sword play.

Nevertheless the past few years have seen a deterioration in the quality of the professional presentations in Peking. In the early 1960s (except for Russian-style ballet which I have mentioned), few countries could match the vitality, originality and, above all, the experimentation of the theatre in Peking. To see the latest dance-drama was one of my special delights, for always in each production there was some new field that the dramatists and performers were exploring. But, owing to the oppressive influence of a few (the Gang of Four), who were in charge of cultural activities, the early 1970s saw a decline in the quality of the professional stage presentations in Peking. A sameness in the themes made theatre-going a far less exciting experience than it had been in the past.

And not only in theatre but in the field of writing, too, this deterioration was noticeable. Anyone who reads the Chinese magazines, or even the reporting in Chinese newspapers, must have noticed how stereotyped much of the writing had become. It seems as if the Chinese, in rejecting the formalism associated with Confucianism and the Chinese classics, succumbed to another kind of formalism based on political orthodoxy. The danger is that stereotyped writing will in the end inevitably lead to stereotyped thinking.

No one was more conscious of this than Mao Tsetung. He said that this style of writing was unsuitable for expressing the revolutionary spirit. 'It is not vigorous, lively, fresh and forceful.' His own writing certainly had these qualities and Mao used to urge people to read Lu Xun (one of the great revolutionary writers) as an example of how to write in a colloquial manner understandable to the common people.

If much of the writing, theatre and films still appear to us to be too stylized, too far removed from natural day-to-day realities, we must remember that the Chinese created these not for us but for themselves, and their cultural 'language' is very different from our own, just as their shared history is very different from ours.

In the early 1970s, however, the Chinese themselves were beginning to complain of the lack of variety. In 1973 Premier Chou En-lai said he had received many complaints and he urged an increase in the number of productions staged. On the stage and in films there was little to see except 'model' revolutionary dramas with their heroic poses and exaggerated language, and there was little characterization in depth. As I write (1978), it appears that fetters are being broken. Films that had been withdrawn are now being released again; artists, writers and dramatists who were ignored or silenced are again being given recognition. With this new freedom I believe we shall see a new and exciting flowering of all cultural activities in China.

In all that I have written so far I have been referring almost entirely to the professional, one might almost say, the official, cultural activities presented in the large cities such as Peking. But of all the writing and painting in China, I have always enjoyed most that done by the simplest and least sophisticated of the people, the peasants. Their work strikes me as being the most direct and least burdened by formal training.

Years ago in a small village, I saw a big notice-board covered with poems written by the peasants of the village, most of them written by people who had only shortly before learned how to read and write. I copied down some of these poems, and here are rough translations of two of them:

Outside the village, peach blossom
opens out; now at this time
commune members work their hardest.
Furrows with the sod turning over
like waves breaking along a beach.
Then in the paddy fields, rows of wheat
being planted out like long arrows,
so swiftly. An eighty-year-old man
insists on coming to work, standing
at night in the middle of the field
holding the light for all to work by.

Drought? but we have
plenty of sweat to spend.
Steep hills? but then
we have lithe legs.
Water too distant? See
how strong are our shoulders.
You old Weather-God,
what can you do to us?*

On our recent journey to Peking, we saw in a Commune a class of
young children outside their village school having a painting lesson. The
paintings have the same quality of freshness as the poems and I reproduce some of them between pp. 122 and 123. Here we see the same
emphasis on group activity, group productive work, the shared life of a
community; and every picture expresses vitality and optimism.

I drew attention at the beginning of this chapter to the astonishing
number of amateur cultural groups of all kinds that have sprung up in
Peking. This is also the case, and has been for some years, across the
whole of China, even in the smallest and most distant villages. What we
are witnessing (and we in the West should remember this before we
make our quick judgments) is something altogether new. It may be that
by our Western cultural standards some of the artistic work is not in our
eyes yet of a very high level, and much of it may be imitative. We must
remember that what we are seeing are factory hands and peasants,
housewives and truck drivers, bank clerks and shop assistants no longer
relying for their culture on the intellectuals of a middle class. The
working people of China are creating their own culture. This has never
happened anywhere else in the world on so vast a scale.

* I also quoted these in my book *The Wall has Two Sides* (Jonathan Cape, 1963).

130

Above, the Universal Chinese sporting slogan; *above right*, volley ball in an open-air stadium; *right*, ice hockey – a relatively new sport in China: a match in the huge National Stadium in Peking. *Below right*, table tennis – the most popular game of all; *below*, at one of the many outdoor swimming pools in Peking.

10 *A Peking Divorce*

To understand how the judicial system in China works we first need to jettison altogether our own concepts of law and legal procedures. As one American judge, George W. Crocket, who visited China in 1975 wrote: 'I quickly learned that my framework [of American criminal jurisprudence] was useless, my concepts irrelevant and the experience ahead of me totally new. To my amazement, I discovered that crime is simply not considered a problem in China.'

To start with, there are almost no full-time, legally trained advocates. When I was in China in 1960 there were only 2,000 lawyers in the whole of China, and the number has been very greatly reduced since then. The few remaining in Peking are mostly occupied with cases involving foreigners. China, unlike the advanced countries of the West, is definitely not a lawyer-ridden society!

The basic philosophic framework for the settlement of all disputes, whether criminal or civil, is to be found in the famous paper written by Mao Tsetung in 1957, 'On the Correct Handling of Contradictions among the People'. Mao separated conflicts into two categories, 'Those between ourselves and the enemy and those among the people themselves.' The 'enemy' Mao defined as 'the social forces and groups which resist the socialist revolution and are hostile to socialism'.

One of two distinct patterns of judicial procedure is followed, according to which of the categories a given offence or conflict belongs. Those involving 'treasonable and counter-revolutionary offences' as well as 'most serious offences' (criminal homicide, brutal rape, robbery, vicious assault or the embezzlement of public funds) are dealt with in formal proceedings with a statement of charges and a trial before a professional tribunal.

The procedure covering conflicts 'between the people' is altogether different. The usual trappings of a formal trial are dispensed with. No lawyers represent the contending parties – they can speak for themselves and they can call on friends, relatives and workmates to speak on their behalf. There are no rules of evidence as we know them, and anything that will aid the court to arrive at the true facts is permitted.

But the most significant contrast between Chinese law and that of most Western countries lies not so much in the outward procedures but in the attitude of the society at large towards those who break the law and towards conflicts arising between individuals.

In civil disputes in the West there is an assumption that one of the parties is in the right and the other in the wrong, and that one of the main purposes of the court is to determine which is which. The contending parties employ highly trained advocates to argue their case, the procedure involving all manner of rules and trappings, ancient legal formulae and rules of evidence that have gradually accumulated through the ages.

The Chinese approach a civil dispute quite differently. The *objective* is different. They know, human nature being what it is, that in disputes between individuals it is only rarely that one party is blameless and the other wholly in the wrong. Thus, the primary aim of a court is not so much to discover which side is right and which wrong (though that, of course, is also considered) but rather to find a way to enable the two disputants to leave the court reconciled and without ill-feeling.

The overwhelming number of disputes do not even reach the lowest courts,* for they are dealt with whenever possible by a neighbourhood 'Conciliation Committee', sometimes called (a very Chinese touch) 'Sunflower Courtyards'. It may seem strange to us that most civil actions can be dealt with informally at the grass-roots level and, more often than not, resolved there. In China, face-to-face or on-the-spot resolutions of conflicts have always been preferred to formal trials and this is one of the old traditions which in a modified form has been carried over to the new China.

Judge George W. Crocket, the American judge whom we have already quoted, summed up his experiences in China in an article in the December 1975 issue of the *Journal of the American Juridicature Society*:

> To understand why serious crime is a rarity, juvenile delinquency nearly non-existent and lawyers virtually unnecessary – it is necessary to appreciate the enormous impact of the new socialist system on every individual in China ...

* There are four levels of courts:
  1 the Magistrate's (or People's) Courts;
  2 the Middle or Regional Courts;
  3 the High Court of a Province (or Administrative Region);
  4 the National Supreme Court.

Children are raised in an atmosphere of social concern. They are enveloped from early childhood with personal attention and solicitude extending from parents to teachers to local officials and to the people themselves. If there is deviant behaviour, the causes are sought in the family or other life experience of the child and remedial action taken. The approach is positive and rehabilitative not disciplinary in a primitive sense.

Those traits we assume to be instinctual – selfishness, greed, the desire to dominate, the compulsion to accumulate – all of these and many other characteristics of our society have no basis for existence in China.

This remarkable absence of interpersonal hostility is epitomized by Chinese police. Their only visible function is to direct traffic. They are casually dressed, are unarmed save for an occasional billy club and are invariably relaxed and courteous. No citizen carries firearms. Jails are few and their population small. The trappings of a restrictive regime are absent. These observations are not only those of casual visitors but have been authenticated by every authority I have consulted or read in recent years.

A *divorce case*

One marital dispute which was not resolved by the neighbourhood 'Sunflower Courtyard' Committee was therefore, at the wife's insistence, referred to a Magistrate's Court. With our friends, Lü and Yu Ma, we went along to see the proceedings. One of the unusual, and in my view eminently sensible, features of the legal proceedings in China is that there are almost no 'court houses' built for the purpose. Cases are tried wherever it is most convenient for those who have to attend. This divorce case was held in the large committee room of the Peking No. 1 Building Material Factory, where both husband and wife worked.

In an adjacent office, we were introduced, before the proceedings began, to the judge, Li Shu-chang, who was the head of the civil cases in the Chong Wen District of Peking. He was formerly a worker and had studied law in his spare time. He spoke quietly, with a certain authority in his manner. An impressive man. We were introduced also to the two assistant judges, a man and a woman, both workers in this factory. To have two lay judges is normal procedure in China, and although the lay judges have no legal training they can out-vote the presiding judge. In this case the two assistant judges had been elected by the factory workers. A young woman was there also to take down the proceedings in shorthand.

I asked the judge whether I could be allowed to photograph the proceedings. He said that as far as taking members of the court was concerned there was no objection, but I would have to ask the couple for their permission too, which I did. While waiting to go into the main room I asked the judge how frequent divorce was in Peking. He said that a poll had recently been taken in one of the five city districts. They found that in two per cent of the marriages one or other partner had formally requested a divorce. Of those who had requested a divorce court hearing between seventy per cent and eighty per cent were reconciled either then or later. It can thus be said that the incidence of divorce in Peking is very low indeed — less than one-half of one per cent.

The following is a brief description of how the case in question proceeded — I am writing from notes which I scribbled at the time and from a transcript which was later made available to me.

The room in which the case was heard is the room normally used by the Management Committee of the factory. A bare room except for a large picture of Mao Tsetung at one end with two of his sayings on either side of the portrait.

The atmosphere was informal but serious. The judges, the married couple and the others — friends and fellow-workers of the couple — were all in their normal working clothes. Most of the men smoked. A mug of tea was set in front of each person, and these were refilled from time to time from thermos flasks brought in by attendants.

The judge, after taking his place, announced that the proceedings were now formally opened. He gave his name, the name of the two assistant judges and that of the woman recorder. He then went on:

> We have come to discuss the case of Meng Tsien-tsung who is thirty-three years old, and his wife, Chang Tsu-lu, who is twenty-eight. It has been clear for some time to their friends and fellow-workers in this factory that something was not going well with their marriage. The leaders in this factory and their friends in the neighbourhood where they live have had discussions with them and tried to reconcile them. When Chang Tsu-lu notified us officially that she wished to have a divorce we made arrangements to convene this court. We have some details about their marriage. They have been married seven years and they have one child who is now three years old.

The judge then addressed himself to the couple, giving them an outline of their legal rights; they could lodge a complaint if they thought the proceedings had been conducted unfairly; they could call on any relatives or friends to speak and if either of them wished to appeal against the decision of the court, they were free to do so and a transcript of the proceedings would be provided for them. The judge's manner while speaking was friendly and direct.

As you, Chang Tsu-lu, are requesting a divorce and your husband wishes the marriage to continue, perhaps you will tell us in your own words why you think your marriage has become unhappy and why you wish it dissolved. There is no hurry. You must take your time and you may tell us anything that you think will help us to understand the difficulties. We are here to listen and if possible to help you both.

The woman then related how she and her husband had met and fallen in love. 'It was a free marriage,' she said — meaning that it had not been arranged by others, which was the old custom and which is still occasionally practised.

At first we loved each other. We helped each other and got along well. But little by little he changed. The main problem is that he thinks men are superior to women and that I should obey him in everything. He doesn't share the household work. I feel he has no confidence in me. Whenever I express an opinion he laughs at me and says I don't know anything. He is also very suspicious. Whenever I laugh with men or walk with another man he thinks I'm having an affair. He often returns home late at night but will never tell me where he has been. His mother makes many difficulties too. She always sides with him and tells me I am not a good wife. It became so bad that last year we separated. I went to my mother's home, taking the child with me. I do not think he wants to change and I see no hope of our marriage becoming a happy one.

She looked intensely sad while she was speaking; she was clearly under great strain.

The man, in contrast, appeared rather cocky and self-confident, and this impression was heightened by his crew-cut hair. He was trying to give the impression, it seemed, of being rather bored, that he had heard it all before. When she had finished, the judge asked him to give his side of the story. He spoke quite briefly. He said he did not want the

136

Above, members of the court; *above right*, the wife, Chang Tsu-lu; *right*, the judge addressing the litigants.

Below, the husband, Meng Tsien-tsung, reading his self-criticism; *below right*, general congratulations at the end of the case.

marriage dissolved. He agreed he had made mistakes but he had never hit his wife, even when she aggravated him with her grievances. Yes, he had been at fault and he would try to be more considerate in the future. 'I still love her and I hope the court will agree that the marriage should be given a further chance.' (As he said this she shook her head vigorously.)

The judge then asked if any of the friends of the couple, or their fellow-workers wished to say anything.

Some of those around the table spoke at length, some quite briefly. The judge occasionally asked a question but otherwise there were no interruptions. The opinions expressed were largely similar – that the man was at fault; that he had a very chauvinistic attitude towards women. Those who had been to their home had noticed that he never helped with the household work or helped with the child. He left everything to her. I felt rather sorry that no one spoke on his behalf. Surely there was *something* to be said on his side. Only the judge, at one point, intervened to say, 'We must remember, all of us, that some people are victims of the old society, that attitudes given them by their parents are difficult to change. We must understand this and not pass judgments too lightly.'

I watched the husband as the quietly spoken criticism flowed on – it must have been for fully an hour. He gradually lost his air of self-confidence. He did not move but stared at the table in front of him. At last, when everyone had spoken, the judge asked him whether he wished to reply. After quite a long pause, the man said, that what had been reported about him had come as a great shock; he had not realized that his behaviour was as bad as they had said. 'I was brought up in a big house when I was small and the women always obeyed the men.' The women also did all the housework, he said, so it never occurred to him that his behaviour was not normal. He asked once more to be given a chance to alter his attitude. At this the woman said, 'These are just words. I do not believe he is sincere.'

Just then, rather surprisingly, the judge called for a recess. He said he wished to speak to the woman alone.

While they were gone, more tea was brought in. There was very little talk. It was as if everyone present was painfully aware that what was being decided that afternoon would deeply affect the future of this small family.

During the recess, which lasted perhaps twenty minutes or so, I noticed the husband writing rapidly and urgently on one sheet after another.

Peking crafts: *left*, decorating fine china, and *above right*, an ivory carving from a Peking workshop.

Restoring an ancient Chinese painting.

Sports and pastimes: *left*, playing Chinese chess; *centre left*, hurdling; and *below left*, a factory group playing basket ball.

Below, practising Tai Chi Chuan in the courtyard of the Temple of Heaven.

The judge and Chang Tsu-lu returned and the room fell silent. The woman had been weeping and she held a handkerchief to her face.

'As you all know,' the judge said, 'it is the policy of our government that everything possible should be done to reconcile marriages when they appear unsuccessful and are creating unhappiness. That is why I called a recess, to see if I could persuade Chang Tsu-lu to accept her husband and give the marriage one more chance. Unfortunately I have failed to persuade her and there is therefore nothing further that this court can do but to accept the situation and to declare that the marriage be annulled.'

The husband then spoke to the judge. 'While you and Tsu-lu were out, I wrote a self-criticism. May I have your permission to read it?' The judge nodded his agreement.

Very quietly the man read from the paper he had been writing. There was no longer a trace of self-confidence in his manner; he looked shattered. For the first time I felt that he was speaking sincerely. 'I wish to thank the court and the comrades around this table for what they have said about me. It is the first time in my life that I have seen myself as I appear to others. I believe they have spoken the truth. I have acted badly and I no longer blame Tsu-lu for wanting to leave me ...' He continued for several minutes in the same strain; his wife was quietly weeping. When he had finished reading he looked up at her and said, 'Please let us try again to make a happy home together.'

The wife made no movement and did not attempt to reply. Very gently the judge asked her, 'Has your husband ever made a self-criticism of this kind before?'

She shook her head.

'It is a big step for him to have taken. Do you think he is speaking sincerely?'

'I do not know. He has said many things before, but never like this and never before other comrades.' She held her head low; her voice was only just audible.

'Do you still love your husband?'

'Yes, I still love him.'

'Then, as judge of this court, I must ask you whether or not you wish to withdraw your application for a divorce. Think carefully and deeply. We will accept whatever you decide.'

The woman said nothing. Her head was still down, her eyes still closed. There was dead silence in the room as we all waited for her reply. Long moments went by. Then at last, her inner struggle over, she looked up at the judge and said, 'I withdraw my application and I will do

139

my best to make the marriage a success. But if it fails I must ask the court to grant me a divorce without any further hearings.' Then looking at her husband across the table she said, 'I think we will succeed.'

The court room sprang into life with an outburst of clapping. The long tension was over and everyone in the room was smiling broadly and laughing. The man looked embarrassed but he, too, had a huge grin. The judge shook hands with the couple and asked them to sign the necessary papers. With this done, and holding hands, the couple walked out of the room and down the passage with others following, shaking their hands and laughing. It was as if they were being married all over again.

Six months later I was once more in Peking.

How were the couple getting along? Had the reconciliation held or had the marriage gone on the rocks again? I had become so involved in that court-room scene that I was most anxious to know how it had all worked out. I was both hopeful and fearful. I asked a friend to make inquiries and I gave him the address of the factory where the couple worked. He returned next day. 'They are happy,' he said. 'They are planning to be at the Summer Palace next Sunday and if you wish to see them they will be at the place where you hire boats. At noon.'

Of course we were there – and so were they, with their three-year-old son. The picture tells the rest ...

11
Some People of Peking

A woman doctor

I'm fifty-one years old; my name is Hu Ya-mei. I have lived half my life
in the old China and half in the new. My father was a capitalist in the
import-export business. I joined the Communist Party when I was
twenty-two — but I had to keep this secret even from my family, for the
Party was illegal. My family was very rich. We had all the comforts we
required. As a daughter of a rich family I had no way out — only to
become a housewife. Women were looked down upon. That's why I
chose to study medicine — to break away from the enclosed circle of the
old society. I was studying at the Peking Medical College during the
Japanese occupation of Peking. After Japan was defeated we all thought
things would get better but they became worse. The Chinese people
became poorer and poorer under the Kuomintang. The terrible thing
was that many people were dying of starvation and illnesses at the same
time that many doctors could find no work after they had graduated
because the people just couldn't pay them. Only the rich. All this led
me to think that merely to treat people was not enough; we had to
arouse the people to change the whole system. It was then that some
of us medical students began to study Marx and Lenin. It was an extraordinary experience, for here at last we had found out the truth — the
way to help China. The Party gave us books and we met in groups,
but always secretly.

The transition in our society has not been easy, especially for us
intellectuals. When we were first sent to the country after the Revolution I found the conditions there very difficult — the food, the dirt — it
was all so different from what we had been used to in the city. I will
never forget that experience; it was a real turning point for me — I began
to see how much the peasants could really teach us, and how deeply we
had been conditioned in a bourgeois way of life. After that I had no
difficulty in adjusting.

141

Left, Hu Ya-mei, a woman doctor; *right*, Wang Yun-man, a factory worker.

A *factory worker*

My name is Wang Yun-man and I'm forty-six. My father was a poor peasant – he worked for a landlord. We were very poor. I had three years of primary school, but I then had to work in the fields for the landlord to help my father make ends meet. At sixteen my father sent me to Peking to be apprenticed – that meant one had to work very hard for almost no pay. That was a very bad time for me. At the time of liberation I heard that there was a shortage of electrical workers so I applied and was taken on. I had to learn how to read and write so that I could understand the work I was doing, so I studied in the evening literacy classes which were then being set up. About seven years ago I became the Director of the Steam Turbine Workshop – you saw the 100,000 kilowatt generators we are making there now. I'm a member of the factory Management Committee but I still work on the factory floor like the others as often as possible. I have very little spare time because we hold most of our management meetings in the evenings. My family? My wife is a worker too, so she understands. We only have to think of the changes that have taken place!

142

One of China's leading painters

My name is Huang Yung-yü — I am a Tu Jai, one of the minority nationalities in China. I was born in 1924 in a very mountainous region. My father was a musician, but he couldn't afford a piano, but he had a harmonium. I had two years of middle school in Fukien. Then I worked for two years at a pottery kiln as an apprentice. That meant I had no wages, but they fed me and cut my hair. I remember that on one occasion they actually gave me a bowl of noodles. I made friends with a primary school teacher and studied woodcuts with him. I had to leave him for his wife kept beating him — they turned out to be members of the Kuomintang. I joined a repertory stage company, painting the back drops. I began to make woodcut paintings and also did some art editing for a newspaper. One teacher I got to know was very good — he was a dramatist, wrote many books, so with his help when I was out of work I would read and this laid the foundation for my classical Chinese.

But I lived haphazardly. In 1939 I joined the Chinese Woodcut Association started by Lu Xun. After wandering around Taiwan and Hong Kong, I returned to Peking in 1953 and became a teacher at the Art College. My troubles began in 1973. The new Peking Hotel was being built and Premier Chou En-lai thought it would be a good idea if the younger Chinese artists would paint original pictures for the many hundreds of rooms. There were quite a number of artists who were invited to do this, but we were informed that the paintings we did were not revolutionary enough — this was the Gang of Four who were opposing anything Premier Chou suggested. They wrote a special complaint about a picture of an owl. That picture was one of mine. Then the Gang of Four put on an exhibition of what they called 'Black Art' and my drawing of the owl was among those criticized. You can't imagine to what lengths they went to attack Chou En-lai — even criticizing the work of the artists he had suggested for the hotel paintings! The reason why the owl was attacked was because my owl had one eye closed (like owls sometimes have). Well, there's an old Chinese saying that if you look at something with one eye shut you don't approve of what you are seeing — so they said that my picture proved that I was against socialism. The other artists were being attacked for equally absurd reasons. We were very puzzled by this at first, until we realized that it was really an attack on Chou En-lai. I was told I was unfit to teach, so I was fired from my teaching job. They kept up my salary, though. We lived in this same courtyard but they reduced our five rooms to two — so my entire family of five had to live in these two small rooms. There wasn't enough room

143

to paint except by rolling up the canvas as I painted. Many friends sent us presents anonymously and expressed their sympathy.

Of course I knew what was going on was wrong and couldn't last but I was afraid they might destroy my paintings so I asked my friends to hide them for me. As a family we had made all kinds of plans in case I was arrested. But instead, the Gang got arrested! You should have seen the excitement and the parties and the fireworks and the dancing when that news came through – you wouldn't believe what a weight it was off all the people.

What are you doing now?

A few of us were asked to make a design for the great tapestry that was to be placed behind the statue of Mao Tsetung in the Memorial Hall. My design was chosen so now forty people are weaving this tapestry – it is very big – about twenty-four metres long by seven metres high. I am going to where they are weaving the tapestry to make sure that the colours are correct. They have given me a studio to work in and soon we shall be out of these two tiny rooms – they are looking for another place for us now. I and my family always knew that things would come out all right in the end. Conditions under the Gang of Four had become impossible – not only for artists and cultural workers but for many others too.

Left, Huang Yung-yü, a leading Chinese painter; *right*, Ma Ching, Chairman of a District Revolutionary Committee.

Chairman of a District Revolutionary Committee*

My name is Ma Ching, and I'm fifty-four years old. I was born in a small village in Shantung Province – my father was a poor peasant.† He is now eighty-four and my mother is seventy-six – they are both still living in the same village. My family was extremely poor and could only afford to send me to school until I was eleven. I've had no further formal education since then, though I have become more literate. My real schooling came from taking part in events and from taking part in the revolutionary movement. I was never a regular member of the army but was a guerrilla fighter – first against the Japanese, then against the Kuomintang. I did a good deal of political work locally among the peasant population, explaining to them what the revolution was aiming to do. Yes, I'm married – my wife works in the East City Revolutionary Committee. I have three children – two are at school, one is in the army. I have been in Peking since 1966 and was elected Chairman eight years ago. You are looking at my bed. The work is very heavy and I am often kept late, so then I sleep here in my office. It saves time.

A soldier

My name is Wang Chung-hsue. I'm twenty-one years old and have been in the P.L.A. for three years. My father was a poor peasant. I grew up helping in the fields, so, during harvest time or when the peasants need us to help them digging irrigation ditches or canals, I find the work quite easy. The army also has its own farms where we grow our own food so that we don't draw on the supplies of the people. The army is basically self-sufficient in grain and vegetables. We have our own pig farms too.

I'm in a division whose main duty is the protection of the capital. It's our job, too, even when we are off duty, to help the old people and the young. We are instructed all the time that we are the servants of the people and not their masters.

Almost every one of us in the army volunteered for the job – many more volunteer than the army needs so I was lucky to get in.

---

*This man's work is the equivalent of a full-time Chairman of, say, Westminster City Council or one of the Boroughs of New York City.
†'Poor peasant' is a specific category. It signifies that the peasant owned no land and had to work either for a landlord or a 'rich peasant'.

Left, Wang Chung-hsue, a soldier; *right*, Kao Min, a welder.

A girl welder at an oil refinery

I'm just twenty-one and my name is Kao Min. I don't know why you are interested in me for I have lived a very ordinary life. I have been a welder for five years and after two years of being an apprentice I became a full worker. My father is an official at a Peking Machinery plant in Peking, my mother is a cadre there, too. I go to see them almost every week-end – the factory runs a special bus for us after work on Saturdays; we stop work early on that day. On other days we work from 7.30 to 11.30, then from 2.30 to 6.30. I earn ¥40 a month (about £13, $25) but living in a dormitory here is very cheap and I never spend all that I earn. I even have a small amount in the bank. I didn't go to senior middle school, just the junior. I don't know why I took up welding as a career – the idea appealed to me so I applied and was taken on. I find it interesting and I'm really glad I chose this work. There's always some-

146

thing new to do. At the moment we are mostly welding pipes here at the oil refinery but sometimes we work on steel girders on new construction projects. The men at first thought women shouldn't do this kind of work, but they take us for granted now. I think we do the work just as well as the men – sometimes I think we do it better!

A chef

I'm a chef at the Chenkiang Restaurant. My name is Kao Kuo-lu. This isn't a very large restaurant – we have seventy people working here and we serve about 1,000 people a day; on holidays and on Sundays it goes up to 1,700 or 1,800. I'm forty years old and only had four years of primary school – that was before liberation, so my educational standard isn't very high. I was sent to Shanghai after liberation to enlarge my knowledge of cooking – that was in 1966. In 1973 they elected me manager. We cater mostly for working people, not many foreigners come here. We are fairly well-known as a fish restaurant, but we make chicken dishes too. We have a buffet, too, where we sell wine and beer. Most of our dishes have the southern flavour – the kind they like in Kansu Province, near Nanking. On average a meal here costs about ¥1 [32p, 60¢] and we are open from six in the morning to eight at night. In summer people drink mostly beer but when it's cold in winter we sell the hot *sauchin* wine.

Left, Kao Kuo-lu, a chef; *right*, a university professor.

147

A *university professor*

I am a professor of electrical engineering and electronic automatic control. I left China the year before liberation and came back in 1955. I was trained at the University of Illinois. It was difficult to adjust to American ways at first – there was a certain amount of discrimination against Chinese – never as much, of course, as against the Negroes. But I remember more than once going into shops where they refused to serve me. After seven years in the United States the adjustment back to China was difficult too; but I was after all coming back to my own country so that adjustment was easier.

I met my wife at the University of Illinois – she is Chinese too. She is now teaching English at a teacher-training school here in Peking.

Yes, I've published a number of books – they are used as text books for the students. I used to play the violin but I don't have much time for that now – though I am still occasionally asked to join musical groups here at Tsinghua.

I look back at my time in the United States with a certain unhappiness. There is so much vitality there, yet they don't seem to know where they are going. It's not a joyful country.

There have been tremendous changes here since the Cultural Revolution, the main change being in the relations between the students and professors. Before, we were very 'professorial' – very aloof from the students. Now we mingle with them more as friends, and they are free to tell us when they think our teaching isn't helpful. It took me quite a time to adjust to this new, freer, more open relationship with the students. It's difficult to change old habits. But the change was necessary – the atmosphere in the universities, and in the schools, is far happier now.

An *instructor at the acrobatic school*

I'm Luo Ping-sung. I have been at this school since it was started in 1954 – I was one of the first students here. I'm thirty-one now and can't do many of the acrobatic turns. I was nine when I began. I had to go through all the basic movements, the tumbling acts, the balancing and so on, just as they do today. Now, as instructor, I go with the troupes when we send them abroad. In 1972 and 1973 we went to eight countries. Yes, I have done most of the numbers – I was a clown, I did a magic turn and I was part of the lion-dance team.

My father was a pedicab driver – that was a terrible job and we were very poor. Eight of us were all dependent on his earnings. It's impossible to describe our life then.

There are twenty-five instructors here now and eighty-eight students – they live in the school. They do their ordinary school work in the mornings and then have four hours of acrobatic training in the afternoon. We provide everything for them – food, clothing, everything. Most of the students are from peasant or worker families. Children apply, but they must also be approved by their fellow class-mates. When they come here for their interviews we give them medical tests and see if they have a natural ability for the work. Of course every city has its own acrobatic school – we are just one of many in China. The youngest of our pupils is eleven.

Left, Luo Ping-sung, an acrobatics instructor; *right*, Kao Chun, a trolley-bus conductress.

A trolley-bus conductress

I'm nineteen. My name is Kao Chun. I have been a conductress for less than a year. I went from middle school to the countryside for a year and a half – to a Commune near Peking. The peasant work was very tiring for us from the city, at least at first, until we got used to it. We had to dig,

149

hoe, pick cotton and dig ditches – everything. I learnt a lot from that experience and I think it prepared me for the work that I am doing now – because this is hard work too. We were trained only for a week – how to give change, how to deal with passengers – especially how to help the old people and the very young. Then I worked alongside an experienced conductress who helped me until I could do it on my own.

What do you do if someone says 'I don't have the money for the fare?'

Well, we are told that our job is to serve the public, so I usually say 'All right, bring it tomorrow if you can.' I would *never* turn somebody off the bus! I would be severely reprimanded if ever I did that! Sometimes – really quite often – when this happens, people send the money to us by post.

Yes, I live with my parents. My father works in the financial section of the Hsinhua News Agency. I have a brother who works in a timber factory and I have an older sister who is in the P.L.A. I'm lucky to have got this job – I really love it.

A typesetter

My name is Yang Teh-shan. My father died when I was nine so I had to find a job to help my mother. I had four years of primary school but didn't learn much there – certainly not enough to become a typesetter. So I first had to become literate during the great literacy campaign after liberation. I now know most of the 5,000–7,000 characters we use in our paper [*The People's Daily*]. I have had a steady job here ever since liberation, starting first as a typesetter apprentice. Ours is not an alphabet language like yours is – that is why we have to be able to pick out by hand each character. The Japanese have mechanized their typesetting, but they use far fewer characters. We are experimenting with mechanized typesetting. Our paper comes out every day, including Sundays and holidays – we rotate our days off. I find I have very little spare time as I need to study so many things which I didn't learn as a child. The total sales of the paper are 4,600,000. It's the official paper of the Party. We send the paper to several other cities by facsimile, so it is read all over the country. It is difficult now to remember the awful conditions in the past. Just think – my eldest daughter is training to be a doctor, my second daughter is a telephone operator. If it had not been for the Revolution my children would never have had the slightest chance to get on like this.

150

Left, Yang Teh-shan, a typesetter; *right*, Wang Wen-chuan, a champion archer.

A *world champion archer*

[This girl broke the world record in 1976 in the seventy metre single-round archery event, with 315 points. The previous record of 310 points was held by the American girl, Miss Myers, since 1974. I had great difficulty in getting her to talk about her achievements.]

My name is Wang Wen-chuan and I'm eighteen years old. I began being interested in archery in Shanghai, where I was brought up. I began in one of the after-school sport centres there. Yes, I have been lucky in breaking some records. I've been quite keen on sports since I was in junior middle school. After graduating from school I spent two years doing manual labour with the peasants in the countryside. My father works at a herbicide factory and my mother in a factory that makes screws. They don't know anything about archery or any other sport, for they never had a chance to take part in sports of any kind when they were young.

151

12 *Last Thoughts*

This book has attempted to describe the capital of a country which comprises a fifth of mankind and which in its new socialist character the West has only recently begun to know.

There is an old saying, exaggerated of course, but which still in a way holds true: 'Once you have lived in Peking you cannot leave it; if you do leave it, you cannot forget it.' The vast majority of Westerners who visit Peking, though this aspect or that might disturb them, are conscious while they are there that they are in touch with a new quality of life, something important and valuable, though they may not be able to name it. I have never myself been to China without feeling that there I breathe a different air. In Peking (and even more markedly in the vast areas of rural China) I am given a foretaste, a hint, of what it will be like one day to live in a classless society. Even now, before that day has arrived, one realizes after a few days, with surprised relief, that most of the ordinary class and money divisions (which we at home take for granted because we are so steeped in them) have disappeared, are gone. Like a noise which one is not aware of until it suddenly stops.

How can a single small book with a few pictures convey the spirit of a huge and complex city? It can't of course. And even to the extent that I have attempted it, can this be considered an objective report? I doubt it, for we can't escape our own nature. Everyone who visits Peking will see the city and its people through his own mental lenses and judge what he sees there according to his own predilections. That I like the Chinese and admire them for their attempts to build a new kind of society must by now be obvious to every reader, so for me to attempt a careful balancing of involvement and detachment would appear as nothing but pretence.

The Chinese, as I have said, have won my respect for their complex struggle to rid themselves of *class*, which includes all the things that divide people from each other. They haven't got there yet, but they are on their way, it's what they are aiming for. This is the vision for which thousands, millions, were ready to give up their lives. You can't be a day in Peking without realizing the confidence and zest with which people look to this future. What a contrast to our apathy and cynicism! Many call their optimism naivety. 'The Chinese will learn one day' – how often I have heard this! – 'that human nature is human nature and they will end up like all the others who have attempted to change society. Give them a few years and they will find themselves ruled by a group of Party hacks with all the prestige- and money-grabbing left unchanged.'

Though history alone will tell, I think these critics are mistaken. The Chinese are very alert to the hidden minefields and dangers along the way, and this awareness itself is half the battle. I have no doubt at all that the Chinese will eventually build the kind of society they want, even if it takes generations, with all manner of reverses and attempted subversion and the need for half a dozen more Cultural Revolutions. The Chinese people in the past quarter of a century appear to have developed a built-in impulse for self-correction. Several times they have drifted away from their socialist objectives, but always with amazing intensity of self-assessment they have rediscovered the right track. The Cultural Revolution was only the most profound and dramatic of these periods of national self-correction and the more recent overthrow of the Gang of Four was another.

As for changing human nature, the Chinese have already demonstrated that people *can* change. There are millions who have entirely shed the effect of their middle-class origins and joined with the rest of the people. No one, I think, should ever underestimate the power of new ideas combined with action – the action needed to meet essential needs; action to understand and correct the unjust power-relationships within a society; and action that adjusts to the objective realities of our environment and our human condition. As Mao Tsetung put it:

> Where do correct ideas come from? Do they drop from the skies? No. Are they innate in the mind? No. They come from social practice and from it alone. They come from three kinds of social practice, the struggle for production, the class struggle, and scientific experiment. It is man's social being that determines his thinking. Once the correct ideas characteristic of the [politically] advanced classes are grasped by the masses, these ideas turn into a material force which changes society and changes the world.

Of course the people of Peking have their problems and anxieties. They were anxious when the Central Committee was split after the death of Mao Tsetung; husbands and wives can be separated by work and see each other only for a few weeks every year; housing shortages often force young people to postpone marriage, and large families must sometimes live in confined quarters. But in spite of this the Chinese have enormous confidence in the future, confidence in the socialist system, and this accounts for much of their sense of ease.

Another reason why the people of Peking walk with such a relaxed and easy step, is that their lives are free of the countless small anxieties that nibble away at our peace of mind: meeting bills with the price of rents, mortgages, food – everything – going up and up and with no end in sight; the problem of the education of our children, especially for the middle class who feel that to give their children a head start they must be sent to a 'proper' school; for many, the fear of the boss and the haunting anxiety of where to turn if they wake one day to find they have no job; and then for so many the looming loneliness in old age. The Chinese are virtually free of all these anxieties.

On the national scale, too, they have managed to avoid the recurrent crises which beset most Western countries. True, the Chinese still have their strenuous internal political struggles from time to time but in spite of these China remains a pillar of stability in today's uncertain world. No inflation, no 'energy crisis', no balance of payments problem, no foreign debt. She feeds herself and exports oil; she has no foreign military bases or troops on foreign soil to give offence to others; and her currency for years has been the most stable in the world. Not a bad record for a country that thirty years ago was known as 'the sick man of Asia', or, in Sun Yat-sen's phrase, 'a dish of loose sand'!

The people of Peking are much, much poorer than the people of London, Paris or New York, but they are more content, they seem to enjoy life more. Most of us surely feel in our bones that we are clinging to a system that is heading towards a dead end. Why are we so reluctant to give up a system that brings us such a complex of personal and national difficulties? Many reasons, of course; but one of them is that we see the enormous effort it will require to change it.

This reminds me of a story told by Lenin about a former Communist who had become a wealthy engineer and was now fearful of a workers' revolution. 'He was willing', said Lenin, 'to accept the social revolution if history were to lead to it in the peaceful, calm, smooth and precise manner of a German express train pulling into a station. A sedate conductor would open the carriage door and announce: "Social Revolution Station! All change!"'*

But as things are moving today we in the West may in any case have to go through a struggle. R. H. Tawney, the historian, put his finger on it:

* Lenin, *Selected Works* (New York International Publishers, 1967).

The most obvious facts are most easily forgotten. Both the existing economic order and too many of the projects advanced for reconstructing it break down through their neglect of the truism that, since even quite common men have souls, no increase in material wealth will compensate them for arrangements which insult their self-respect and impair their freedom. A reasonable estimate of economic organization must allow for the fact that, unless industry is to be paralysed by recurrent revolts on the part of outraged human nature, it must satisfy criteria which are not purely economic.*

China knows that common men have souls; indeed (as I hope this book has shown) it is the common man himself that is making the new society. The Chinese simply do not accept the assumption on which we base our system — that the restless search for wealth and possessions, or 'getting ahead of others', which we call success, will ever bring peace of mind. They do not measure the degree of civilization by material wealth but by the quality of their relations with each other, for it is in relationship that men find all that is most precious and tender in life, and what we call 'success' is often only another form of personal disaster.

When I'm in Peking I feel a painful nostalgia for the sense of community which we in the West have all but lost. There I find myself among a people knit close by a thousand invisible threads of respect and liking, creating a social climate in which there is no need to be competitive or pretentious. Even I, a stranger among them, am affected by this almost tangible atmosphere of mutual trust; it communicates itself to me so that I find that little by little my own inveterate defensiveness diminishes. That is why I always find it so hard to leave.

But leave eventually we had to, and the day of our departure arrived. Yu Ma, Lü, Ch'i Ming-tsung and one or two other friends took us to the airport. We got there far too early, as one always does in Peking, so we took a few last photographs of each other among the flower beds outside the airport entrance and then went in to have breakfast in the airport restaurant. We did not do much talking. While at breakfast a message for me was broadcast on the loud-speaker system and Lü went out to see what it was. It was from the hotel. 'Mr Greene left a ball-point pen in his room. Shall we send it to the airport by car or keep it until he comes to Peking again?'

'Lü,' I said, 'ask them to keep it for my return.' It seemed a good omen.

* R. H. Tawney, *Religion and the Rise of Capitalism* (Penguin, 1969).

A Few Facts and Figures

Everything changes fast in Peking. Here I list a few of the more interesting figures most recently available (1976). To show how rapidly the city is developing I have, in some cases, included figures of a few years earlier. Comparative figures for London, New York, Tokyo, are for 1976.

GEOGRAPHIC POSITION
40° North (approximately on the same parallel as Southern Italy and Philadelphia).

AREA OF GREATER PEKING
16,800 square kilometres (Greater London: 986 square kilometres; Greater New York: 483 square kilometres).

POPULATION
8 million (London: 7 million; New York: 7½ million; Tokyo: 11½ million).

POPULATION INCREASE (BIRTHS OVER DEATHS)
0·958 per cent (Chinese national average estimated at 1·8 per cent).

INFANT MORTALITY
In urban Peking: 10·35 per 1,000 live births.
In rural Peking: 15·7 per 1,000 live births.

MEDICAL FACILITIES
28,710 hospital beds (24,000 in 1974): i.e. 1 hospital bed per 279 of the population.

Medical personnel
22,684 fully trained doctors (1974: 15,686).
15,226 para-medical personnel (Barefoot-Doctors) in rural areas (1974: 13,800).
19,314 'red medical workers' in the city, (equivalent to the Barefoot-Doctors in rural areas) (1974: 8,000).

COST OF MEDICAL SERVICES

In urban Peking: free for all students and staff at schools and universities, members of institutes and all government workers.

Those who work in mines, factories, etc., are fully protected by their organizations' medical plans.

All children and other dependants pay half. The average cost of staying in hospital for those not covered is 30p (57¢) per day plus 15p (28¢) per day for food.

Maximum cost of major operations for those not covered: £2.45 ($4.65).

In rural Peking: peasants join a co-operative medical plan costing 30–50p (57–95¢) per head per year. This covers peasants and their families for all medical services.

COST OF MEDICINES

Prices dropped by an average of 82·1 per cent between 1952 and 1976.

INCIDENCE OF DISEASE

Smallpox, plague, cholera, typhus and venereal disease – eliminated; diphtheria, whooping cough, measles, polio, typhoid – 'under control'.

MAIN MEDICAL PROBLEM

Geriatric medicine, owing to greatly lengthened life expectancy.

EDUCATION

Kindergartens: 4,486 with 230,000 children (in 1975, 1,000 with 120,000 children).

Primary schools: 4,830 with 830,000 pupils (in 1974, 5,025 with 1·12 million pupils).

Middle schools: 1,221 with 1·26 million pupils (in 1974, 927 with 900,000 pupils).

Total number of children at school in Peking: 2·12 million – 26·5 per cent of the total population.

BANK DEPOSITS	1976	1974
	¥724·14 million	¥625·00 million

FOOD CONSUMPTION		
Meat	320·73m. *jin*	226m. *jin*
Fish	104·42m. *jin*	87m. *jin*
Eggs	41·17m. dozen	38m. dozen
Vegetables	24,232m. *jin*	20,034m. *jin*
Sugar	69,788 tonnes	68,000 tonnes

PEKING

	1976	1974
CONSUMER GOODS SOLD		
Bicycles	242,371	225,000
Wrist watches	427,911	243,000
Radio sets	353,455	239,000
Sewing machines	85,211	87,000
NUMBER OF SHOPS, MARKETS, ETC.	14,703	10,900
NUMBER OF HOTELS		
Large hotels	8	no change
Smaller hotels	156	179
Restaurants	1,013	800
Hotels used by foreigners	4	4

SOME CONVERSIONS
¥ *(yuan)* 1 = 32p, 60¢
1 *fen* = 0·32p, 0·6¢
1 *jin* = 0·5 kilo

Index

159